FLEXIBLE SPECIALIZATION

FLEXIBLE SPECIALIZATION

The dynamics of small-scale industries in the South

Edited by
POUL OVE PEDERSEN, ARNI SVERRISSON
and MEINE PIETER VAN DIJK

INTERMEDIATE TECHNOLOGY PUBLICATIONS 1994

IT Publications Ltd,
103–105 Southampton Row, London WC1B 4HH

A CIP catalogue record for this book
is available from the British Library

ISBN 1 85339 217 0

Typeset by Dorwyn Ltd, Rowlands Castle, Hants
Printed by BPC Wheatons, Exeter

Contents

Preface

Flexible specialization, new competition and industrial districts are some of the many terms used to refer to the dynamics of small enterprises. Usually the terms are put forward in the context of developed countries, but questions also arise in Eastern Europe and the South: what determines the dynamics of the industrial sector? Which role do small enterprises play in this sector? How can we achieve that kind of dynamic development?

Since its inception, the EADI Working Group on industrialization strategies has had the potential of small manufacturing enterprises in the South as one of its main concerns.[1] Since the general conference of EADI in Oslo in 1990, efforts have been under way to apply the concept of flexible specialization and use network theories to understand the problems of small industries in the South and study diffusion of innovations in small enterprise environments.

The authors contributing to this volume have worked within this context. Flexible specialization has been accepted as a concept generating relevant topics for research. The results are presented in the papers in this volume. Earlier versions were discussed during a workshop at the Research Policy Institute in Lund. Topics taken up are the importance of flexible production techniques for small industries in the South, of clusters, of interfirm linkages, of trading and other networks, of technological development and an advanced division of labour, and the collective efficiency resulting from this. A number of the subsequent chapters are critical about the flexible specialization concept and draw on a wider range of theoretical traditions to explain the dynamics of small enterprises.

P.O. PEDERSEN
A. SVERRISSON
M.P. VAN DIJK

1 Introduction

Industrialization in the North created what has come to be called 'Fordism', referring to the assembly-line technology that played an important role in the success of the T-Ford automobile production at the beginning of this century. The Fordist type of production organization is usually coupled with 'Taylorism' in management. This implies a clear line of command, and a highly-developed division of labour and stratification within the factory, which places management and workers on different sides. This has been seen as a fundamental weakness of many Western economies by many critics, e.g. Best (1990). Furthermore, the Fordist paradigm has come under criticism in the wake of increasing difficulties in balancing an economic scale of assembly-line production with existing consumer demand.

Hence, elements of a post-Fordist industrial paradigm have emerged in the wake of economic troubles in the seventies and the eighties. The central feature of this discourse is the emphasis given to increasing flexibility. In developed countries this means automation, electronic information systems and robotization. In addition, neo-Fordism is based on semi-autonomous groups of producers, often small firms. Their co-ordination depends on a centralized information system, which is often located within an established corporation. Through this form of organization, producers are able to respond efficiently to fluctuations in the volume and quality of sophisticated and differentiated consumer demand.

These developments have also suggested that industrialization does not necessarily have to mean an increasing share of mass production in large-scale enterprises. Indeed, the flexible specialization concept puts small industries at the centre of the industrial strategy debate. Piore and Sabel (1984) suggested that the deterioration in industrial performance in a number of Western countries results from the limits of the mass production model and saw flexible specialization as a future alternative. They emphasized in particular the decentralization of big factory chains and redeployment of productive forces in small units, which take advantage of flexible technologies. Dissolution of rigid mass production systems and introduction of more innovative ways of producing, using multi-purpose equipment and employing skilled workers, would enable crisis-ridden economies to react to continuous changes.

Schmitz (1989) explicitly discussed the applicability of these ideas to the Third World. He distinguished a small enterprise variant and a large firm variant of flexible specialization. In the first case, flexible specialization results from the clustering of small firms and a strong interfirm division of labour. The large firm variant exists when large firms decentralize and specialize internally or use specialized suppliers. The latter in particular has produced organizational innovations such as 'Just In Time' (JIT) inventory management techniques.

The small-firm variant of flexible specialization presumes that clusters of small producers can reach collective efficiency. Innovative behaviour is expected in such an environment and competition is tempered by co-operation. Suppliers of parts in the automobile industry can and do compete, for example, but co-operation between the 'assembling' firm and its suppliers, or between suppliers, in solving specific technological problems, also occurs.

Clustering of enterprises can enhance this co-operation and help the enterprises in surviving economic adversity by increasing their capacity to adapt to changes in the environment. In many cases small enterprise clusters are not only able to survive during hard times, but actually increase their share of total production, at the expense of mass producers (Piore and Sabel, 1984:12). This has *inter alia* been demonstrated by their ability to withstand and respond to the oil and debt crises.

The problem remains of how to measure flexibility, innovative mentality and collective efficiency. The last concept can easily be confused with localization, urbanization or other agglomeration economies.[1] Innovativeness and flexibility at the level of enterprise clusters are not as easy to identify in the field. Several papers in this volume, however, suggest different approaches to this problem.

Enterprise environments and collective efficiency

A key element in the theory of flexible specialization is the realization that the individual enterprise cannot be understood in isolation from the specific environment in which it is operated. Both the structure and the efficiency of the enterprise depend on the products and services available from other private or public enterprises in the area, on the structure and qualifications of the labour force, and on the size and structure of the market. Agglomerations of differentiated interacting activities may achieve what Schmitz (1990) has called collective efficiency. The areas where they are clustered are often called Marshallian (industrial) districts after the English economist Marshall who wrote about such districts in the beginning of the twentieth century (see Pyke, Becattini and Sengenberger, 1990; and Pyke and Sengenberger, 1992).

If needed services or production inputs are not available on the market the enterprise will either have to produce them itself, accept an often much-reduced efficiency, or choose a technology which reduces its needs for external inputs. The choice of technology also depends on the structure of the labour market, and the choice of product depends on the size and structure of the market.

Flexibility in a production system is a response to instability and uncertainty in the market (Salais and Storper, 1992). Large-scale production requires a relatively large and stable market to be profitable. To secure the necessary market stability, large-scale producers are forced to opt out of the smallest and most unstable markets and leave them to niche producers, to subcontractors or un-serviced.

Enterprises venturing into these smaller and more unstable markets have, briefly, three options:

- They may invest in multipurpose machinery and employ skilled labour which make it possible for them to shift production between different markets and thus create stability for themselves, although their individual markets may fluctuate. This option corresponds to what has come to be known as flexible specialization, or what Pyke and Sengenberger (1992) call the 'high road' to industrial restructuring.
- They may minimize their investments in machinery (and preferably treat investments as sunk costs) and rely on unskilled labour which can be hired and fired at short notice. In this way the enterprise may be able to survive, although its market fluctuates wildly. This option leads to what could be called sweatshops often operated as simple subcontractors. It corresponds to what Pyke and Sengenberger (1992) call the 'low road' to industrial restructuring.
- Finally, in the smallest and most unstable markets, very small or household-based enterprises may survive on a semi-subsistence level. Capital investment is insignificant, and only part of the labour of the proprietor and family is devoted to the venture, which is supplemented by other sources of income from agriculture or formal or informal wage labour.

These options form a hierarchy with respect to size, capital intensity, productivity and market. The competitiveness of each option depends not only on output market structure, but also on labour markets, input markets and the general social context in which the enterprises operate. Examples of each will be given in the following chapters.

Flexibility of labour markets

For the large capital-intensive enterprise, stability of the labour force, especially but not only in the higher echelons, is important for stable production and high-capacity utilization. The needed qualifications will often be highly specialized and enterprise specific, and in order to reduce the costs of training and labour turnover the enterprise will often train people so narrowly that their qualifications cannot be utilized in other enterprises. On the other hand, it will also be willing to pay above average wages in order to keep its trained personnel. Thus the enterprise will attempt to create an internal labour market where the enterprise and at least its core personnel have a common interest in reducing labour turnover.

Enterprises choosing the flexible specialization strategy will require a core labour force with broader and more general qualifications. However, it will be relatively easy for the qualified workers to switch from one enterprise to another. Therefore, the enterprises will also be unwilling to finance training, which is rather paid by the trainees themselves or by the government. On the other hand the high mobility of labour is important for rapid innovation diffusion among the enterprises and it will often be relatively easy for workers to start their own enterprises.

Enterprises choosing a sweatshop strategy will typically offer relatively poor working conditions, low wages and unstable employment. However, even in the sweatshop, on the job training is often important, and although the enterprises hire and fire workers according to seasonal and cyclical demand, the same workers may often be attached to the enterprise for long periods. Especially in rural areas there may be a mutual interest in such permanent seasonal employment if it complements the agricultural work seasons.

Finally, the very small semi-subsistence enterprise will typically offer employment only to the owner and possibly to some family members. It will often be a part-time activity supplementing agricultural work or some type of wage work. The incomes earned in such activities vary widely depending on the activity, the qualifications of the owners, their investments and the priority they are able and willing to give to the enterprise.

In principle, all four enterprise strategies are likely to be pursued in any society. However, the importance of each strategy will vary, depending on the character of local and global markets and their accessibility. The larger the accessible market, the more important will the mass production sector be.

The growing importance of flexible specialization

In the industrialized societies, flexible specialization is often said to have become more important partly because the market for more specialized high-income consumer goods has expanded and partly because subcontracting and what has been called 'labour market informalization' has become increasingly important. However, the increased demand for small and medium-scale flexible production is also a more direct result of the development of large-scale production itself; firstly, because large-scale production requires more standardization which increases the demand for niche products to cover markets which cannot be satisfied by the standardized product. Secondly, with increasing levels of mechanization and automation the large-scale producer needs a growing supply of dedicated, non-standard machinery and equipment to maintain and renew the production system.

In the developing countries the situation is very different. Markets are significantly smaller and less stable. Consequently, the room for large-scale production is much smaller than in the industrialized countries. In spite of this, the goal of industrialization policies in many developing countries has been to develop large-scale industries. Supported by government and donor funds, production capacity has in many cases been expanded well beyond the feasible level. This has resulted in low capacity utilization, which the government has attempted to increase by granting monopoly status to these companies. Instances of preferential treatment in allocation of scarce resources and foreign currency also abound, and outright state ownership is common in many countries. This strategy has effectively blocked the development of other alternatives. Semi-subsistence producers and small workshops have remained at that level, and frequently suffer from harrassment by the authorities.

The absence of small-scale service establishments and input suppliers in the local environment has often led large enterprises to develop such auxiliary activities within the enterprise. Such activities are usually not operated at an optimal level and this therefore further reduces the efficiency of the large enterprise at the same time as they undercut the chances for developing such activities on a market basis.

As a result, the intermediate enterprises which do develop tend to grow out of the demands of the semi-subsistence producers and consumers, rather than as a response to the large-scale sector. However, their development is limited by the low purchasing power of their main customers, and they are unable to break out of this vicious circle because of the closed, monolithic and monopolistic nature of the mass-production sector, and the attractiveness of its products for the local elites, middle classes and labour aristocracy. Expansion therefore tends to create sweatshop groups, rather than flexibly specialized enterprise networks.

Because of this, it can be difficult to distinguish between nascent flexible specialization and proliferation of sweatshops. They coexist side by side, and only a closer look at their operations will reveal which trend is dominant. Where flexible production and Marshallian districts could be said to exist it is often at the same level as or at an even lower level in terms of wages, skills and employment security than the sweatshops. This problem is discussed in several contributions below, but particularly by Knorringa and Wilson. Furthermore, Cho shows that even South Korea, which started its industrialization on the basis of very large-scale production, has developed a production system during the 1980s based on a mix of large-scale production, flexible specialization, and sweatshops, particularly in the garment sector.

Lastly, low-income levels and instability in the economy often force people to rely for their survival not on one activity, but on a mix of wage labour and entrepreneurial activities in small or large enterprises. Their association to labour market organizations and unions, therefore, tends to become rather unclear, while on the other hand social and family networks become more important. For small entrepreneurs the result is often that they are only able to focus part of their energy and resources on their enterprise and, therefore, are also less likely to succeed.

The new competition and flexible specialization

Best sets himself the task of integrating 'a theoretical analysis of the business enterprise with extra-firm concepts of markets, competition, regulation, and planning that have been the preserve of economists' (1990: viii). He uses the term the 'new competition' to refer to the prevalence of firms that are organized to 'pursue strategies of continuous improvement in product and process within a regulatory framework that encourages industrial restructuring' (Best, 1990: 252). The emergence of this phenomenon has increased pressures on firms everywhere to reorganize or restructure their operations.[2]

Best's book addresses the failure of the United Kingdom and the United States to compete with Japan, the newly industrializing countries (NICs) and some European countries. His main point is that big business in the United States suffers from rigid command structures and control routines in production organizations, and he calls for restructuring according to the organizational principles of his theory.

At the centre of this paradigm is the entrepreneurial firm; 'an enterprise that is organized from top to bottom to pursue continuous improvement in methods, products and processes' (ibid: 2).[3] Such firms seek a competitive edge by superior product design (which may or may not lead to lower costs) and organizational flexibility, which manifests itself in a variety of interfirm complexes, ranging from groups of small Italian firms linked by co-operative associations for joint marketing, technological advance and financial underwriting, to giant Japanese organizational structures co-ordinating trading companies, banks and manufacturing enterprises.[4] Such firms will also try to capture export markets where possible and Best argues that the emergence of the 'new competition' has taken the United Kingdom and the United States by surprise.

The new competition concept contrasts with the old competition concept, which was predicated on mass production at the lowest cost possible. The old competition was 'market-coordinated by vertically specialized industrial enterprises' (ibid: 7), whereas the new competition turns on strategic action, which aims at the shaping of markets, in contrast to responses in reaction to markets. The new competition is distinguished from the old in four dimensions:

1. *The organization of the firm.* It has a strategic orientation to choose the terrain on which to compete, while the traditional, hierarchical firm takes the terrain as given. The entrepreneurial firm actively seeks a strategic advantage.

2. *The co-ordination of phases of production in the production chain.* The choice is not restricted to plan, market or hierarchy. Consultative–co-operative interfirm relations may exist among mutually interdependent firms.[5]
3. *The organization of a branch of activity.*[6] This refers to a variety of interfirm practices and extra-firm agencies such as trade associations, apprenticeship programmes, labour education facilities, joint marketing arrangements and regulatory commissions, each facilitating interfirm co-operation.[7]
4. *Patterns of industrial policy.* According to Best, the health of an industrial system depends on combining competition with co-operation. This can only be achieved by policy intervention. Industrial policies should help to shape markets and address production rather than distribution and be strategically focused.

However, the new competition does not necessary affect all sectors of the economy. Traditional non-exporting sectors may be less affected in particular by the developments discussed above. Another criticism is that Best does not explain why all of a sudden the new competition emerged.[8]

The 'new competition' concept is more general than the flexible specialization concept, which explains the success of industries in Italy, Japan and Germany that are based on craftsmanship, multi-purpose equipment, industrial districts and networks of innovating entrepreneurs. These are also the essential elements of any strategy based on that theory. The flexible specialization theory focuses primarily on firms interacting with other firms and the way they use their technologies. In contrast, the new competition theory looks at worldwide markets and emphasizes primarily the different modes of organization that are possible in branches where vertical disintegration is the trend at the moment (for example the automobile and electronics industry).[9] The key variables in the flexible specialization theory are technology and division of labour, while the new competition theory stresses improvements in methods, products and processes, including organizational forms, financial arrangements and marketing strategies. Increased research on the organizational and institutional aspects of flexible production is therefore necessary, and can be initiated by drawing on the new competition theory.

Both theories include a spectrum of strategic factors. Among these are the importance of continuous alertness, the combination of some competition with some collaboration and the advantages of subcontracting relations. Policies in the case of flexible specialization concentrate on creating clusters and networks and an environment prone to innovation, while the new competition theory stresses the importance of shaping markets and of targeting strategic sectors. Government policies should have a production focus and encourage firms to seek strategic alliances.

Technological change and technological networks

To assess the dynamic role of small and medium enterprises in the future and to delineate growth paths open to them, it is necessary to examine specifically their technological characteristics and those of enterprise networks, although it is not only technology which contributes to flexibility. Employment of casual labour, piecework contracts and product diversification are also among the strategies used.

It is important to consider technologies as integral parts of social networks, and transcend the dichotomy common in the popular literature between technology and society. After all, technology refers not only to the 'hardware' used in production, but also the organization of production processes, the knowledge applied, etc. (Callon, 1987; Sverrisson, 1993).

Any production process can be analysed as a series of more or less well-defined steps. Every step can be carried out within the confines of a single enterprise, or they can be developed as specialties of separate but interdependent enterprises. The former is typical of 'mass-production' enterprises of the old variety, as well as the large-scale variant of flexible specialization. The small and medium-scale variant, however, implies the subdivision of the process, involving several enterprises. Further, if each step is carried out by autonomous enterprises, and moreover, several enterprises are capable of the operations necessary for each step, an enterprise network is needed to ensure the co-ordination of the entire process.

Let us consider the consequences of this for technological change, and first address the options within each enterprise. In ordinary furniture production, for example, the main production sequences is as follows: sawing, planing, cutting of joints, sanding, joining and varnishing. Each step in this and most other production processes can be carried out by the means of handtools, and these are moreover often the property of the workers, and do not belong to the enterprise or its proprietor. However, each step can also be mechanized, or a mechanized function such as turning can be introduced, without the simultaneous mechanization of other operations. In this way it is possible for a handtool-based enterprise to develop along a path of incremental mechanization towards a fully mechanized workshop. The changes implied by increasing mechanization in the organization of the work are minimal. An example of this is provided in Sverrisson's paper below. This possibility is also in line with the limits on available capital in most small and medium-scale enterprises, making it all the more tempting for the proprietors.

However, any process of the type described above needs raw material and inputs, and distribution and transport are commonly separate functions carried out by specialized enterprises. Hence, the production of furniture can also be considered as an interactive process involving several enterprises. They may be involved in forestry, lumbering, saw-milling, furniture manufacture, transport or sales. One production unit could conceivably do all this. However, usually several enterprises perform each of the functions mentioned and if one does not deliver, the manufacturers simply go to another. This contingency of relations within interactive enterprise networks are the key to other aspects, such as adaptability and innovativeness.

From the analysis above, it can for example be seen that flexibility in a network or enterprise collective is increased as the production process is separated into ever smaller parts, each organized in an independent unit. This is particularly relevant in the case of gradual mechanization. In order to mechanize, say planing, in a carpentry network, each enterprise does not need a planer. It is sufficient that one enterprise possesses a planer, if (and only if) this enterprise in turn provides planing services to other enterprises. This happens often enough, and similar relationships can be based on any other power tool, machine, or technically-defined segment of the production process. A mechanized spinning factory may for example provide thread to weavers using hand-operated looms, which in turn can sell the cloth to all kinds of enterprises, including household-based, rural dressmakers. The possibility of combining technology sophistication levels in other words also exists on the level of branches of industry.

Usually then, each enterprise involved in a production process has a specialized function of some kind. Exactly how the lines are drawn depends on the context: in Africa, the possession of a woodlathe is enough to set up a specialized turning shop because this tool, common though it is, is not found in the majority of carpentry enterprises. Simultaneously, cylindrical legs are very popular in many countries. If tastes were different or capital more plentiful, the lathe could not have this significance.

Arrangements of this kind maximize the benefits of partial mechanization of the network. However, to be effective the different parts of any production network must be closely attuned to each other, and this can *inter alia* be accomplished through the design of the hardware, by building an integrated production plant. The Achilles' heel of this type of integration is, however, that bottlenecks somewhere in the production sequence hold up the entire plant. If the process is prone to such bottlenecks, this can easily lead to a situation where any benefits which might accrue from scale economies are erased.

Technological and social networks

An alternative mode of integration is social rather than technical. The different phases in the production sequence can be matched by subsuming them under one management, or alternatively, through the activities of brokers or traders of various descriptions, or to use Williamson's terms, through hierarchies or markets. In actual fact, of course, existing networks combine these types of co-ordination mechanisms.

Which particular combination prevails, however, has direct implications for technology choice, and the other way around: available technologies may preclude certain social arrangements and preselect others. The former has been the case in small enterprise networks all over the Third World, where divisible techniques and multi-purpose machinery is the rule simply because it fits the bill. The converse has occurred in numerous technology transfer projects, in which large-scale plant has been installed, in which the different steps in the process are not only organizationally, but also technically integrated. Attempts must also been made to line up suppliers and distributors in order to cater for the demands imposed the aim of running this particular plant effectively (Bagachwa, 1992). This in turn has called for a replication of the crisis-ridden corporate bureaucracies of the North, but this time in the South, where the immanent weaknesses of this type of organization are amplified, in particular by the absence of the infrastructure which they presuppose.

We saw above that the technical characteristics of the production sequence in many small and medium-sized enterprises in the South facilitate gradual mechanization. In addition, social aspects such as poverty increase the attractiveness of gradual and flexible mechanization, rather than the promotion of integrated mass production systems (see Kaplinski, 1990; Smillie, 1991). However, flexible specialization implies more than this, namely the co-operation of enterprises in some form.

The network approach makes it possible to elaborate this, otherwise underdeveloped, aspect of the flexible specialization theory. This approach has *inter alia* been refined in a series of Swedish innovation studies (Hakansson, 1987; Laage-Hellman, 1989). A network is then seen as a series of units which are interconnected through varied types of social relations. There is commodity exchange, information exchange, exchange of services, subcontracting, mutual reliance on technical specifications or standards, a common labour force, a common language, a common location, a common social background and so on. Such social production units are not fixed entities and their relations, technological and others, are not completely determined by the network. Hence, such technological networks are conceived to be in a state of constant evolution. Their borders are indeterminate and changing and the roles of different units in the networks are likewise malleable.

This in turn explains the innovative potential of certain participants in such networks, as well as the evolutionary potential of the enterprise networks themselves. If they are compared to a technically-integrated production system, a central characteristic emerges. It is possible for a unit in a loosely-integrated technological network to change its role, by launching a new product, introducing a new machine, or whatever, without the whole network having to follow suit immediately. Hence, experimentation is possible without jeopardizing the network itself. After all, most of the units will carry on with business as usual. If the experiment turns out well, it is likely, of course, that the innovator will be imitated by his peers, and a diffusion process results. If, however, the experiment fails, no great harm is done, and the resources of the network, never committed in their entirety to the experiment, are largely intact. Under these circumstances, the risk for the production collective as a whole is significantly less than when this collective is closely integrated by hardware design, detailed technical specifications, and other sources of scale economies.[10]

These processes are particularly relevant to the problems of enterprise collectives in the South. There, experimentation usually means being the first to introduce a technique, which is mature in and of itself, and make it work in the local social context.[11] However, this type of development potential can only be realized in the case of innovations, which possess either or both of the following risk-minimizing characteristics:

- They are divisible. This is typical of the introduction of new input into an existing production process: the introduction of veneered blockboard or other similar material instead of massive wood can proceed gradually in a furniture workshop.
- They are of a multi-purpose character or, which amounts to the same, are single-function techniques. A drill can be used to make holes in just about any material, more or less effectively, but then, it is limited to this particular function.

The network argument reveals the close correspondence called for between technique and organization, if both are to function well.

Spatial elements: locations, clusters and industrial districts

Under certain circumstances some local regions and towns, especially in the industrialized countries, have become dominated by enterprises following one of the strategies discussed above and developed into a:

- Fordist industrial centre, or a 'one-company' town;
- Marshallian district;
- sweatshop economy; or
- semi-subsistence economy.

In these cases, enterprise structures, private and public services, labour markets and social networks may over time have adapted to each other and their environment and merged into mutual symbiotic patterns of social reproduction. Even enterprises which elsewhere would follow a strategy other than the dominant one, tend to take colour after the dominant strategy in order to exploit the collective efficiency of the local environment. Such arrangements persist as long as they offer viable solutions to the problems of survival even for the poor in an otherwise hostile economic environment. Therefore they may also be very difficult to change when conditions change. Vested interests have developed which defend the *status quo*.

For a peripheral region it is obviously easier, although not very attractive, to end up as a semi-subsistence or sweatshop economy, than it is to develop into a Fordist centre or a Marshallian district. On the other hand, for a peripheral centre to be based on a few large mass production enterprises is not very attractive either. Such large enterprises tend to develop relatively few local linkages and therefore small local multipliers. In addition they have no desire to train a labour force with broad qualifications which could attract new competitors on the labour market.

Flexible specialization and the Marshallian district may arise both through upgrading and diversification of the sweatshop economy and by decentralization of large enterprises, which simultaneously shed various auxiliary activities. This transformation, however, is in neither case an easy process. Developing the close-knit economic, social and political structures characterizing a Marshallian district is a long and tortuous process. Such production systems based on flexible specialization have so far primarily been described in the industrialized countries. However, as shown in the contributions to this volume, similar phenomena are frequently found in the developing and newly industrialized countries (see Rasmussen *et al.*, 1992). However, empirically they exist rather as combinations of the types suggested above, where enterprises following different strategies mingle. This is borne out by almost every paper in this volume.

Agglomerations of differentiated interacting enterprises may, however, achieve collective efficiency, even if they are not fully-fledged Marshallian districts. In much of the literature on flexible specialization such collective efficiency is understood to be found in areas characterized by agglomerations of small and medium-sized interacting enterprises engaged in the same differentiated production complex, producing primarily for a non-local market. However, although most of the literature stresses the local and equitable nature of the enterprise networks found in Marshallian districts, there is reason to emphasize that such local networks are usually linked up to larger national or international networks which are hierarchical rather than equitable. The modern Marshallian district will typically be subcontracting intermediate goods to large national or international industries or producing consumer goods for large export/import agents, wholesalers or retail chains, and it will often depend on resources or components provided by other large companies.

The rediscovery of the Marshallian district appears to fill the void created in discussions about regional development when the growth centre theory was discarded around 1970. Both theories focus on the initiation of local growth and development and both stress the importance of innovation and change, but they also differ in important ways. Where the growth centre theory, especially in its practical applications, focuses on large-scale industries, the Marshallian district is based on small and intermediate enterprises. Where the growth centre theory emphasized scale economies, the theory of the Marshallian district emphasizes diversification and flexibility. Where the growth centre theory was concerned with intersectoral linkages, the collective efficiency of the Marshallian district is based on intrasectoral linkages. Finally, the social structure and social networks play a much larger role in the theory of the Marshallian district than they did in the growth centre theory.

Main research issues

No agreement on a common definition of flexible specialization has been reached by the contributors to this volume. From the ongoing discussion a number of issues has emerged, however, which it is worthwhile to study in detail.

The first issue is whether mass production and flexible specialization are mutually exclusive alternatives, or whether these two types of production organization and the techniques corresponding to each of them can co-exist for longer or shorter periods. Pedersen contends that mass production does inevitably create opportunities for niche-oriented, flexibly-organized production, because standardized products do not satisfy everybody's needs and preferences. Sverrisson maintains similarly that mass production and flexible production are likely to co-exist, rather than out-compete each other, particularly during the initial phase of the industrialization process, because of the different socio-economic basis of each of the two types of production system. Further Knorringa's and Cho's case studies on India and Korea respectively, and Wilson's study of the Mexican garment industry all document the co-existence of different technology levels and forms of enterprise organization, suggesting a similar conclusion on this issue.

Another problem is the role of brokers and middlemen such as traders in small enterprise networks. It is obvious that such networks can only develop with difficulty if all participants are simultaneously engaged in production and marketing. Goods also need to be transported and distributed, and some kind of finance, formal or informal credit, will be essential in many cases. Several papers focus on this issue, which is more explicitly addressed in Weijland's contribution.

A third concern is the role clustering actually plays in facilitating division of labour, diffusion of technical information, and other kinds of co-operation between enterprises, leading to higher overall efficiency. This discussion links naturally with evaluation of various industrial estate experiments in developing countries. The problem is further analysed by Van Dijk on the basis of research in Burkina Faso and Indonesia, and by Rabellotti on the basis of data from Mexico.

The fourth issue is the types of networks linking small enterprises. Subcontracting networks which link different enterprise cultures are the main subject of Cho's paper on enterprise networks linking large and small enterprises in Korea. However, the limitations of this approach are brought out clearly in Knorringa's paper on the footwear industry in Agra (India). Absence or the incomplete character of such links is also a major concern in the African case studies.

The fifth issue is the diffusion of technical innovations and the consequent increases in productivity. This is the main theme of Sverrisson's contribution. Reorganization of enterprise networks is also analysed as an integral part of the innovation process in Sandee's discussion of tile producers in Indonesia.

Lastly, the benefits to workers and working proprietors as well as the sacrifices entailed by small manufacturing enterprises are discussed in a number of papers. This issue is in particular central to Wilson's analysis of current trends in the Mexican garment industry.

An interdisciplinary approach

The contributors to this volume come from a number of academic disciplines such as geography, sociology, business administration and economics. All authors bring into the discussion the distinct concerns of the traditions in which they are trained, tempered by research work in the field. The papers published here therefore bear witness to the fruitfulness of interdisciplinary discussion and co-operation conducted in a spirit of mutual respect and appreciation of the contribution each academic specialty has to offer in the study of small-scale industrialization. This leaves unresolved however how the current discussion about flexible specialization, industrial districts and industrial networks in the South is related to theoretical innovations appearing in the various disciplines in recent years.

Among geographers working in this area, the spatial configuration of enterprise networks and the predominance of enterprise links within local communities *versus* between such communities and national centres and the global economy have naturally been in focus. In order to study this aspect concretely, it has been necessary to reconsider the role of small and intermediate-sized towns as the loci of industrialization processes and to consider the positive contributions enterprises in such locations can make to development. In this discussion both the links with the rural hinterland and links to trading and processing enterprises in national centres of economic activity are important. No less important, however, has been the ability of enterprises to develop certain production activities collectively, through co-operation, and to adapt to changing relationships between global and local markets, in a manner generally associated with the flexible specialization perspective, but also developed within discourses about innovation networks. These issues are discussed most explicitly in Pedersen's contribution but are also central in the contributions of Cho, Knorringa and Wilson.

From the sociological perspective, economic interaction usually appears in the guise of personal rather than spatial networks (Scott, 1988). Small enterprises are consequently conceived primarily as the ambit of the economic activities of particular persons, the enterpreneurs. In so far as enterprises are seen as organizations interacting within a network, a conceptualization shared by both geographers, sociologists and business economists, the emphasis is on a variety of personal relationships occurring in the interstices of formal organizations. This in turn has been a central concern of the proponents of the flexible specialization thesis (e.g. Hirst and Zeitlin, 1991).

Drawing on current neo-functionalist approaches to social systems, small enterprise networks can be seen as highly volatile, indeed at times chaotic, but nevertheless identifiable and continuously functioning entities. In these networks, manufacturing entrepreneurs associate with workers, traders and other participants in utilizing available and adaptable techniques, thus forming a collective production unit or a 'meta-enterprise', the scope of which goes beyond the individual enterprise as commonly understood in the literature. This makes it possible to grasp within one theoretical framework the well-known multitude of enterprise forms occurring in the South. More specifically, they can be analysed in terms of stabilization mechanisms, central and peripheral actors, different types of exchange and interaction occurring over and above elementary commercial transactions, and the consequences of this for enterprise growth and technological change. This approach is most consciously used in Sverrisson's paper to analyse gradual diffusion of intermediate technologies. However, similar problems are prominent in Sandee's and Weijland's contributions.

From an economic perspective, the main challenge to the flexible specialization thesis is the new competition concept. Van Dijk argues, on the basis of his studies in Indonesia and Burkina Faso, that the new competition approach has three advantages. Firstly, technologies and innovations are defined more broadly than by the proponents of the flexible specialization thesis and the new competition paradigm highlights more adequately the importance of organizational innovations. Secondly, the new competition considers a wider array of organizational forms than most discussions of flexible specialization where subcontracting arrangements are often seen as the paradigmatic form. Strategic alliances, co-operative competition and non-hierarchical networking among firms of equal status are among the options available. Thirdly, due to this, marketing, export co-operation and the creative utilization of market segmentation are considered quite as important as flexibility, general adaptability and technological innovation.

Each of these approaches has important methodological consequences. The emphasis in this volume is on micro-level and locally-oriented studies. These can be conducted as surveys, as reported for example in the contributions of Van Dijk, Knorringa, Rabellotti and Weijland, or as series of systematic case studies such as presented in Sandee's and Sverrisson's papers. However, it is important to relate the findings of this type of research to macro issues, a challenge taken up particularly by Cho, Pedersen and Wilson.

Within this general context it is obvious, however, that in concrete research projects, the emphasis will always be on one aspect or another of the flexible specialization and innovation network problematique. The strength of theoretical paradigms depends, after all, mainly on their capacity to generate directions for research, hypotheses as well as more diffuse ideas, to be tested in the field. Further, in providing guidelines for the reconstruction of analogous processes in one country after another, such paradigms facilitate cumulative production of communicable knowledge, rather than mere accumulation of disparate cases studies. In this respect, the flexible specialization thesis and related discourses have been found to be quite promising.

Conclusion

What are the prospects for flexible specialization in the South? Some of the contributors, such as Knorringa and Wilson, are pessimistic. Competition and differentiation within small enterprise collectives and power struggles are seen as obstacles to co-operation between the enterprises. Others, such as Sandee, note that co-operation is in many cases a prerequisite of technological innovation. Whichever position is taken, it is clear that the fate of small and intermediate enterprise networks cannot be separated from short-term conjunctures any more than they can be discussed without reference to secular trends.

From the vantage point of Southern governments and donor organizations, the main conclusion is that a new approach is needed in order to facilitate enterprise co-operation in small enterprise environments. However, it is also important to avoid over-generalized prescriptions. As yet, the discussion about flexible specialization and innovation networks in the South suffers from both conceptual underdevelopment and a relative scarcity of relevant cases studies and surveys. The appropriate roles for policymakers on the one hand, and practitioners in the field and non-government organizations on the other hand, are by no means clear.

Government and interfirm organizations will, however, have to play a much more active role in the flexible specialization environment than in the large-scale and sweatshop environment. Government and interfirm organizations will be important especially in vocational training, development and transfer of new technology, and perhaps in some cases, in providing the organizational framework needed to harvest the fruits of collective efficiency. It is no coincidence that the role of local governments in the developed countries in enterprise support has been increasing since the 1970s, concurrently with the growth of flexible specialization.

Further, the World Bank's present insistence that governments in the developing countries should concentrate on providing universal basis education and leave vocational training to the enterprises is cast in doubt if flexible specialization is seen as a realistic alternative. In the long run, such a policy is likely to support the already-existing industrial structure based on sweatshops using unskilled labour and large enterprises based on narrow internal training.

There is no doubt that the potential for development through small and intermediate enterprises exists in many cases. However, it is equally obvious that severe obstacles have prevented that potential to be realized in the past to the full extent possible. Indeed, many enterprise collectives seem to be caught in a vicious circle of relative stagnation. However, it is the hope of the editors as well as of the other contributors that the studies contained in this volume can help to suggest the means to escape from this situation.

AFRICAN CASES

2 Structural adjustment and the structure of the economy of small towns in Zimbabwe

POUL OVE PEDERSEN

Rural industrialization: Consolidation of rural non-farm activities – decentralization of urban industries

This paper focuses on small rural towns as intermediaries between the rural economies on the one hand and the formal, mainly urban-based, national industry on the other.

The development of small towns themselves depends on their ability to develop this intermediary function in commerce, services and production. Equally importantly, their intermediary function means that both positive and negative effects on the rural areas of structural adjustment and other economic policies to a large extent are channelled throught the activities in the small towns. Therefore, the effect on rural development of such policies can only be understood on the basis of knowledge of the structure and development of the economy of small rural towns and their linkages to both rural areas and larger urban centres.

However, most research on economic and industrial development has taken a purely national perspective. It has mostly been based on statistics of the formal industry, which treat the industrial sectors as homogeneous. If the informal sector is considered at all, it is also mostly looked at as more or less homogeneous. Although it is increasingly realized that there are important interactions between the formal and informal sectors, the perception of both formal and informal industrial sectors as homogeneous makes it impossible to understand the nature of these interactions, which often take place between formal and informal activities within each industrial sector. As a result, one of the serious deficiencies of the structural adjustment and other economic policies is our inability to take account of their effect on the rural/informal economy.

Similarly, most rural research in Africa has, since the 1970s, looked at the rural areas as a whole without distinguishing the specific role which small towns play in rural industrialization and development. Although the rural centres in Africa usually do not weigh heavily in terms of neither population nor rural non-farm activities, most of the larger and growing activities are located there. It is difficult to see how the rural areas can be industrialized without development of the small towns. So much of the development effort in Africa and also in Zimbabwe has focused, on the one hand, on the large-scale urban-based industry and, on the other hand, on the very small-scale, often rural, semi-subsistence sector. There have been both theoretical and ideological reasons for this and governments, donors and NGOs are basically all agreed. But the result has been that the possibilities for developing those market-based intermediate enterprises,[1] on which a rural industrialization must be based, have been highly restricted.

In order to understand the mechanisms of small-town growth as well as the way small towns function as centres of transmission of development (or exploitation) between the urban and rural areas, the Centre for Development Research (CDR) in Copenhagen has carried out research on small towns in Africa during the last four years. This paper summarizes some of this research especially concerned with the district service centres or rural growth points in Zimbabwe.

The second and third sections of the paper present the theoretical and empirical approach to the research. From a national perspective the three industrial sectors which have been selected for detailed research are then presented, and the final sections analyse the three sectors from a small-town perspective.

The conclusion discusses the impact of the structural adjustment policies on rural industrial and commercial development on the basis of the three sectoral studies. Finally, we question one of the main assumptions implicit in the structural adjustment policies, namely that they eventually will lead to the creation of homogeneous and stable markets.

Theoretical approach

Theoretically, our research builds on a *network concept of the enterprise* which is related both to the Scandinavian network approach (see Johanson and Mattson, 1986; Christensen *et al.*, 1990; and Pedersen, 1989) and to the Anglo-Saxon theory of flexible specialization (see Schmitz, 1990; Aeroe, 1992; Rasmussen, 1992a; and Rasmussen, Schmitz and Van Dijk, 1992).

This network concept of the enterprise differs from both:

- *the neoclassical microeconomic concept of an enterprise*, which conceives of both small and large enterprises as an independent economic unit which on the basis of a certain production machinery produces goods or services for an impersonal homogeneous market, where all the enterprises operate on equal terms and where price and quantity are the only interesting variables;
- *the petty commodity production concept* where the small enterprise is seen as marginalized, operating on markets with a cut-throat competition and no possibility ever to advance in an economy dominated by large national and international enterprises and their branches. As a result, the focus tends to be on income and employment generation rather than on production, and although the small enterprise sector is often seen as an integrated

part of the production system, its importance is usually seen in terms of labour reproduction rather than in terms of production itself.

In the network approach to the small enterprise, which is used in our research, the small enterprise is seen neither as completely dependent nor as independent, but as a node in a network of enterprises where it is linked to other enterprises both public and private, large and small. These linkages may be in terms of flows of goods, money and information, but also in a dynamic sense, in the form of change and adaptation to other enterprises in the network. In such a process of mutual adaptation, each enterprise attempts to find its own specialized niche in the network, where it is able to survive and possibly grow. This leads to a process of specialization and market segmentation which one can see the beginning of in the small African towns we have been studying.

In this dynamic network of interacting and interadapting enterprises and organizations, some relations may be pure market relations, others strictly hierarchical power relations, but most are likely to be somewhere in between, implying some degree of trust and reciprocity, because the market is seldom purely anonymous and the powerful seldom almighty.

Empirical approach

Empirically, this enterprise concept means that we firstly *a priori* assume that all enterprises are directly interdependent of each other and not just interacting via the market as assumed by the neoclassical and petty commodity enterprise concepts. It is through this interdependency that collective efficiency as described in the flexible specialization literature (see Schmitz, 1990; and Pedersen, 1989) may or may not be realized. It implies that although we have been interviewing enterprises, it is the small-town production and service environment as a whole rather than the individual enterprises which comprise our object of study.

Secondly, we assume *a priori* a much larger differentiation and diversification among enterprises and the functions they perform than is implied by concepts as petty commodity producers and formal–informal sector dichotomies. But we also include a much broader spectrum of activities in our enterprises concept than the production enterprises on which many small enterprise studies have focused. Thus we include:

- both commercial and production enterprises partly because they are typically competing about the same local market, and partly because most small production enterprises are in fact retailers as much as they are producers;
- both formally-independent local enterprises and branches of non-local private or parastatal enterprises. We perceive of both as local enterprises albeit with different degrees of independence. Small formally-

independent enterprises are often highly dependent on larger enterprises, while branches may have considerable degree of freedom, depending on the corporate management policies;

- both private enterprises and local public offices as actors in the local economy. In much traditional thinking, a local planning office or other public sector office would be seen as an administrative unit carrying out decisions made in the ministry. We shall rather conceive of it as an independent decision unit which of course to a larger or smaller extent is bound by central decisions, but which still has considerable scope for local action, if it dares to use it.

Finally, although we have been studying the local small-town economy, we have not only looked at the local linkages. In fact, the local economy of the towns we have been studying is rather fragmented and cannot be understood without understanding the way it is linked to the higher levels of the urban hierarchy as well as to the rural areas.

On the other hand, even though there are few direct linkages between local enterprises, this does not mean that there is no local interaction. Rather there is a process of market segmentation going on, where the enterprises adapt to each other trying to find niches in the local market where they can exploit their own advantages in terms of quality of product, price, location, delivery services, credit, family and social relations.

In order to obtain a detailed picture of the local economy and its linkages to the national economy we have chosen to focus on a number of specific sectors including input and machinery supplies, services and other activities related to the sector. Thus one could say that our studies have been focusing on specific sectors in the national economy, but from the perspective of small town.

We have chosen to look at three sectors which make up an important part of the small-town economy, namely:

- the agricultural marketing and processing sector,
- the building sector including building material production and trade, and
- the clothing sector.

As we shall show below, the three sectors are very differently structured and thus national policies are likely to have a different impact on each.

Geographically the building sector study was carried out in the district service centres of Gutu and Murewa, while the two other sector studies were carried out in Gutu and Gokwe district service centres. Our presentation here will primarily be based on data from Gutu with sideviews to Gokwe and Murewa.

Gutu centre is one of the largest of the district service centres. It has a population of around 20,000 and is located 225km south of Harare. Gokwe and Murewa centres are a little smaller, and located 300km west and 70km east of Harare, respectively.

The three sectors in the national economy

Agricultural processing and marketing

Agroprocessing is one of the largest industries in Zimbabwe. According to Riddell (1990) the formal food, beverages and tobacco industry employed 39,200 people in 1983. This figure has probably increased since then but we have no data on this.

In addition to these formal industries, there are around 60,000 small food-processing enterprises (with less than 50 employees, but an average employment of only 1.85) according to a recent survey of small enterprises in Zimbabwe (GEMINI, 1991). Almost 50,000 of these, however, brew traditional beer, while small butcheries, mills and bakeries only make up around 12,000 enterprises with a total employment of probably around 20,000. Practically all these small enterprises in the sector are located in the rural areas.

Finally, there is a large number of rural vendors and retailers trading in farm products and livestock, according to GEMINI around 75,000 enterprises, with a likely employment of about 140,000.

Building

The formal construction sector has, through the 1980s, employed 40–50,000 people (Republic of Zimbabwe, 1991). Most of them have been employed by large companies, mostly located in the large towns, but some also operate outside. In addition to this, there is also considerable employment in building material production and trade in the formal sector. This subsector cannot be isolated in the statistics but a qualified guess of its employment may be around 20,000.[2]

Besides this formal building sector, there is a large small-scale building sector. According to GEMINI (1991) there are around 35,000 small construction enterprises with less than 50 employees, and in addition around 45,000 carpenters, welders, brickmakers, masons, and hardware dealers which are mostly engaged in the building sector. Most of these enterprises are located in the rural areas. Together these enterprises in the small-scale building sector probably employ around 150,000 people, or more than twice as many as the formal sector.

Clothing

The clothing industry has, since Independence, been one of the most important and rapidly-growing manufacturing industries in Zimbabwe with a considerable export. The formal industry consists of 240 enterprises (with more than five employees) with a total of 24,000 employees (December 1991; since then it has been declining). Employment, however, is strongly concentrated, as 22,000 of the employees are employed in the 73 enterprises which are members of the Zimbabwe Clothing Council. These 73 enterprises thus have an average employment of 300, while the rest of the enterprises in the formal industry only have an average employment of 12. Only 25 of the largest enterprises are responsible for almost all the export.

The formal part of the industry, however, only makes up a small part of the total clothing sector. According to GEMINI (1991) there are an estimated 170,000 small enterprises (with fewer than 50 employees) in the clothing sector (tailoring, dressmaking and knitting) with an average employment of less than 1.5 and thus a total employment of around 250,000. Little is known about the productivity and production of these small enterprises, but in average it is much lower than in the large industry.

In addition to these manufacturing enterprises, there is also a large number of retail and wholesale businesses in the clothing sector. According to GEMINI there are around 30,000 small clothing vendors and retailers in the country.

The structure of the three sectors in summary

The data presented above show that the small enterprises are important in all of the three sectors, although not equally important:

- Agricultural processing and marketing has, as in many other African countries, been highly centralized. It has been dominated by parastatals and large private food-processing plants, while small-scale activities (except for beer brewing) are relatively scarce.
- The building sector, on the other hand, is more decentralized, with relatively many small enterprises, builders, carpenters, welders, brickmakers etc.
- Finally, the clothing industry makes up a position in between, with an important private large-scale sector but also an even larger small-scale sector.

These sectoral differences are even more pronounced on the subsector level. Small and large-scale activities are within each sector linked together by processes of specialization, competition, market segmentation and supply–demand relations. For each of the three sectors we shall in the next three sections investigate these processes in more detail from a small town perspective.

Agricultural processing and marketing in the small town economy[3]

Although one should expect agroprocessing to play an important role in the economy of small towns, this has for historical reasons not been so. Until Independence in 1980, agriculture in the communal areas was mainly based on subsistence. Very little of the agricultural produce in the communal areas was marketed and the market for processed agricultural products was even smaller. The bulk of commercially-grown farm products were grown in the white farming areas and consumed in the larger towns. Therefore, there was a certain rationale for centralizing the processing industry in the large towns. Since Independence this has, however, changed. The new government has, with considerable success, attempted to integrate the communal areas into the market economy by extending the marketing, extension, and financial services into the communal areas. As a result more than half of the marketed maize and cotton was produced in the communal areas by the end of the 1980s.

This growing commercialization of the rural economy, together with an extension of public services (especially education and health), has led to a growth of the small towns and a rapid expansion in the demand for commercial food products (and also other industrial products, especially clothing and building materials). In the district service centres and other small rural centres, this has led to a rapid growth in private shops and parastatal marketing depots, but only slowly in processing activities. As a result, most of the agricultural products are transported to the large towns to be processed, at the same time as the small towns are being supplied with commercial food products from the large towns.

Figure 2.1 shows a diagram of the agroindustrial complex as seen from a district service centre in 1990. It is based mainly on data from Gutu/Mpandawana. The activities shown in bold letters are activities found in Gutu centre. The rest are large town activities on which Gutu depends.

The core of the system, and one of the largest local activities, is the depot of the Grain Marketing Board (GMB), which has a monopoly both on exporting grain and oilseeds out of the communal area and on selling grain and oilseeds to local processing industries.

GMB's most important buyers are the large milling companies, breweries and oil extractors located in the large towns. Only a few percentages of the marketed products are sold to local processing industries.

The small rural grinding mills (of which there are also some in Gutu centre) are only service mills which usually do not trade in grain. However, since the mid-1980s, there has been a small commercial roller mill in Gutu. It was established by one of the large milling companies to produce mealy meal and maize flour, but it has had difficulties in getting into the local market and, therefore, has had to distribute to a much larger area than originally intended. As a branch it never became a good business, and in 1991 it was sold to a large private business.

A small part of the maize flour from the mill was sold to the local bakery, a branch of a large chain of bakeries. Most of the input to the bakery, however, is wheat which is not produced locally.

Before Independence there was a *chibuku* (local beer) brewery in Gutu, but it was closed down already before Independence. Today there are only depots of the large national *chibuku* and beer breweries, which as we saw

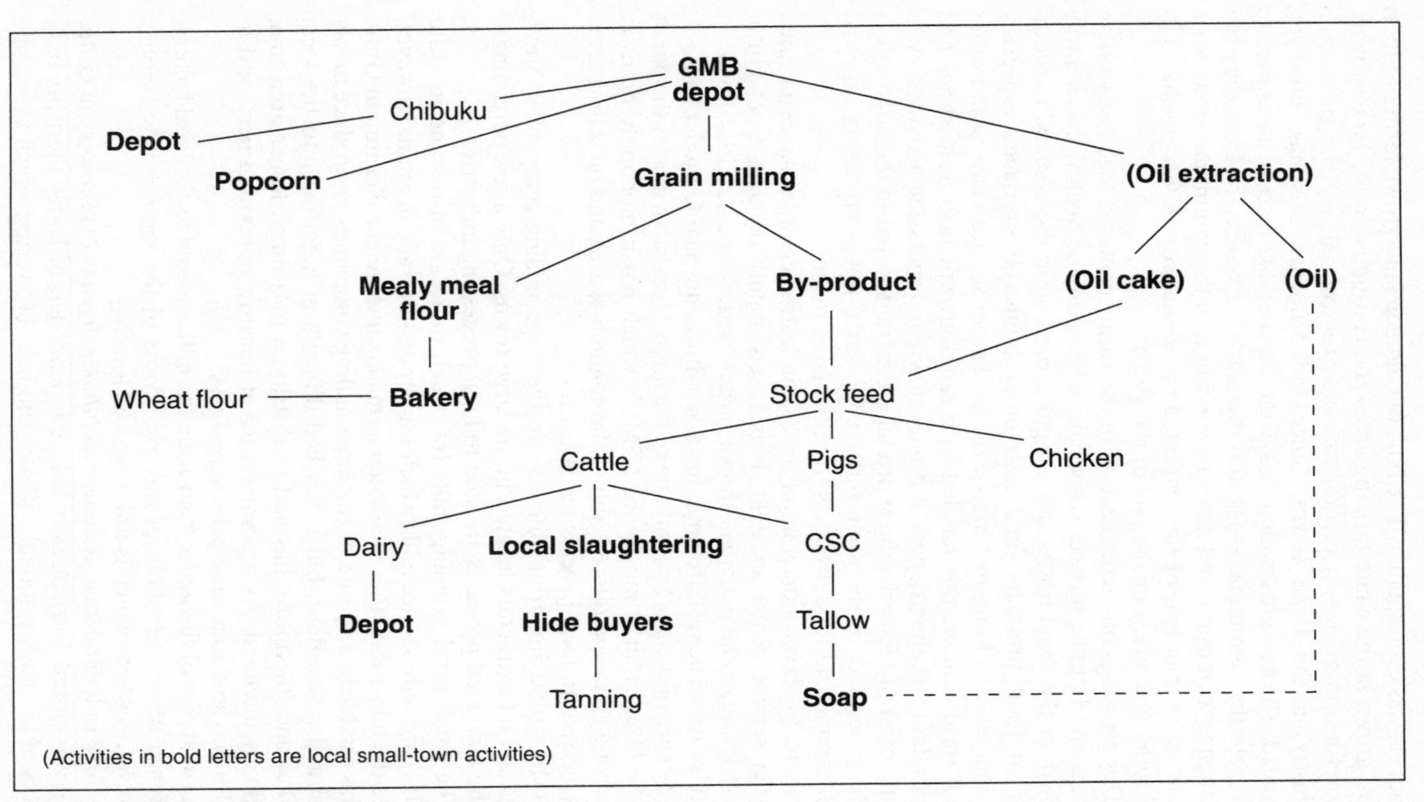

Figure 2.1 *Agroprocessing and marketing*

above have to compete with a very large and probably growing amount of small-scale brewing in the rural areas.

Finally, there is a small popcorn production unit (attached to the local soap factory) which buys its maize from GMB.

No oil extraction was carried out in Gutu in 1990, but there were plans to make an oil extraction plant, and such a plant was opened in 1991 by a local businessman.

There is a large number of cattle in the communal areas. They are, however, mostly slaughtered and sold locally or used for subsistence. Very few reach the commercial meat market, partly because they are often in a very poor condition. Butcheries, even in the rural areas, are therefore supplied either from commercial farms or mostly from the Cold Storage Commission which has had a semi-monopoly on commercial cattle slaughtering.

The locally-slaughtered cattle provide hides which are bought by hide merchants either through travelling buyers or (in Gokwe) through a local branch office. However, tallow, which is an important input in the production of cheap soap, is only produced by the large abattoirs and, therefore, is periodically in short supply. The small soap factories existing both in Gutu and Gokwe suffer from this periodic lack of tallow supplies, which on the other hand means that when they are able to get tallow they have no difficulties in selling their soap.

Finally the local milk production is very small, and very little of it reaches the commercial market. Nearly all the commercially-sold milk products are supplied by the Dairy Marketing Board (DMB), which in 1990 had a depot in Gutu and a recently-opened one in Gokwe. Practically all the raw milk processed by DMB is produced by the large commercial farms.

The main difficulty in developing the agroprocessing activities in the small towns is the parastatal pricing policies. Since long before Independence, GMB has been buying grain and oil seeds at a fixed price at the depot gate. This practice was not changed after Independence, but the network of depots was extended with many new depots in the communal areas. This has given the small communal farmers access to the commercial market, but also increased GMB's transport and administration costs and, therefore, gradually its deficit. This pricing policy has undoubtedly been the main cause for the rapid expansion of commercial agriculture in the communal areas during the 1980s and, therefore, highly beneficial to rural and small town development.

On the other hand, towards the processing industries GMB has also operated a policy of fixed selling prices at the nearest depot, and that has been problematic. This selling-price policy has meant that small processing industries which only need small local supplies have had to buy their inputs at the same price as large processing industries which depend on supplies from a large part of the country. Consequently, GMB has indirectly subsidized the large industry with free transport and made it difficult for the small to compete, because they obviously have higher processing costs and should survive on their small collection and distribution costs.

Another problem for the small commercial processing industries in the small towns is related to the by-products of the milling process, which are important for their production economy. In grain milling the by-product makes up 20 to 25 per cent of the grain input and in oil extraction 65 to 75 per cent. These by-products go into stockfeed production. However, as oilcake was not originally produced in Gutu, the grain by-products have had to be shipped at high costs to Harare or other large towns where a stockfeed production takes place. On the one hand, this reduces the profitability of the small mills. On the other hand, the strong concentration of the processing industry leads to a concentration of the stockfeed production which means that the price of stockfeed (of which the collection cost is subsidized by GMB, but which has to bear its own distribution costs) in the peripheral parts of the country becomes prohibitively high and therefore the demand for stockfeed is low. Thus, the indirect subsidy to the large urban processing industry is likely to delay the development of a marketable livestock production in the communal areas.

The building sector (including building material production and trade) in the small town economy[4]

In the small-town building sector, small local and large non-local enterprises compete on the market. The building sector enterprises located in the small towns consist of:

- local, mostly small, registered contractors;
- local builders and building co-operatives;
- a number of different specialized artisans: plumbers, electricians, painters, carpenters, welders, brickmakers and masons;
- local hardware and general dealer stores selling building materials;
- branches of non-local building material merchants.

However, at the same time, the local market is also supplied by large non-local registered contractors and non-local building material producers or merchants distributing directly to the small towns and their rural hinterland.

There is considerable market segmentation in the building market and the different types of enterprises tend to serve different parts of the market. Roughly the market can be divided into three sections:

- Institutional and parastatal buildings which require public tenders are practically all carried out by large non-local contractors or public building companies. Although some of the small local contractors technically might be able to carry out some of these large projects, they are usually unable to provide security for the often large amounts of capital needed. In addition in periods of unstable supplies they will often be unable to purchase the building materials required for such contracts.

- Shops and modern high-cost housing are built by local contractors. Much of the high-cost housing built for public or parastatal civil servants during the 1980s, however, was built by large non-local contractors because they were tendered out in large projects covering a large number of houses.
- Finally most of the low-cost urban and traditional rural housing is undertaken by small builders, building co-operatives or building artisans. The artisans may be subcontracted or employed by the contractors or builders, but in low-cost housing they will often be hired directly by the house owner who then often participates in the building process himself. Other artisans, especially carpenters, welders and brickmakers, engage fully or partly in the production of building materials or furniture.

Although the small local enterprises play a larger role in the building sector than in agroprocessing, the large non-local contractors have dominated the small town market for modern buildings, especially those built by the public and parastatal organization. This is partly due to tendering practices which have not been favourable to the small enterprises.

During the early 1980s, the government made some attempts to engage small local builders and contractors and also to establish local building co-operatives. However, in general the results were not encouraging, because the local contractors too often were neither good nor reliable enough, and by the end of the 1980s these attempts had almost stopped.

The development of small artisan workshops in the district service centres appears to depend very much on the local building regulations and by-laws and their administration. Strict zoning regulations, lack of small plots and high building standards often require small businessmen to invest an excessive amount of money in buildings before they are able to invest in production and machinery. However, there appear to be big differences from town to town, e.g. conditions for small enterprises seem to be more favourable in Gokwe than in Gutu.

This increased need for capital is further aggravated by the difficulties of obtaining loans. Until recently, land in Zimbabwe's small towns could not be bought, but only obtained on one-year leaseholds. Although leases were usually renewed automatically, it has not been possible to use such leaseholds as collateral for loans. This has recently changed, but lack of surveyors means that it will take some time before the reform is carried out.

This inability to use land as collateral has of course been a problem for all businessmen in the small towns; however, it has hit the building sector

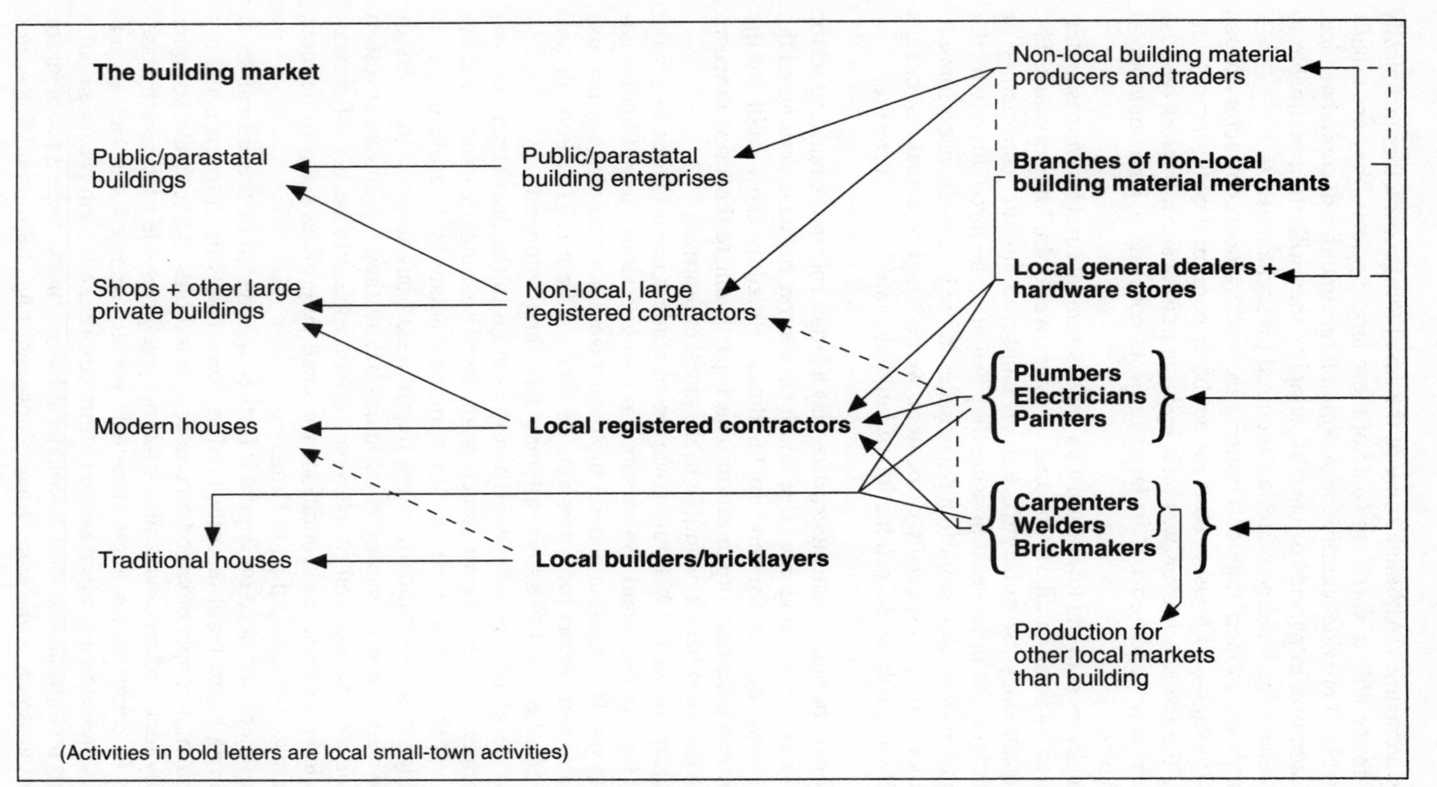

Figure 2.2 *The building and building material sector*

more seriously than other sectors because it has made the financing of new buildings difficult.

The building material market is dominated by standardized mass-produced items distributed both by local building material dealers and by non-local merchants and their travelling salesmen or local branch outlets. There is fierce price competition but also a certain market segmentation, not built so much on product differentiation as on differences in delivery services (transport, outlet location, credit, and product availability). Still some small local producers manage to compete. By selling directly from the workshop they have very low distribution costs; often they also produce a lower quality and, therefore, cheaper product. However, the increasing demand has initiated a certain product specialization where the small workshop produces custom-made window frames, burglar bars or specialized building blocks, which the large enterprises do not produce.

The clothing sector in the small town economy[5]

In contrast to the small-scale agroprocessing and building sectors which are mostly rural, less than 50 per cent of the small-scale clothing sector is rural.

The supply of clothes for the small-town market is dominated by retail trade and especially by branches of large national retail chains (in both Gutu and Gokwe there are more than ten chain stores selling clothes), but also locally-owned clothes shops and general dealers selling some clothes and fabric.

There is a certain segmentation of the market both according to income groups and types of clothes. Most of the chain stores cater for the middle income groups. In Gokwe (which has a higher income level than Gutu) some of the chain stores specifically cater for the high income groups (civil servants and traders). They sell higher quality goods at higher prices and typically give credit. In Gutu some of the local shops perform that role. Many of the general dealers and some of the locally-owned shops rather cater for the middle to lower income groups.

School uniforms are an important market segment which most shops try to serve but in which one chain in particular has specialized. A special small market now developing is the market for sports clothes. In Gokwe a very small retailer has specialized in sports clothes, and in Gutu a new large book-binding enterprise with 30 employees, rebinding old books for the school, prints school names and logos on T-shirts for the schools' sports teams as a sideline activity.

The chain stores are supplied with almost all goods from their head offices and usually have no competence to buy on their own. The locally-owned shops and general dealers are mostly supplied by wholesalers or producers in the larger towns, although some of them, especially those catering for the low income market, get their products directly from small workshops, often through family relations in the larger towns.

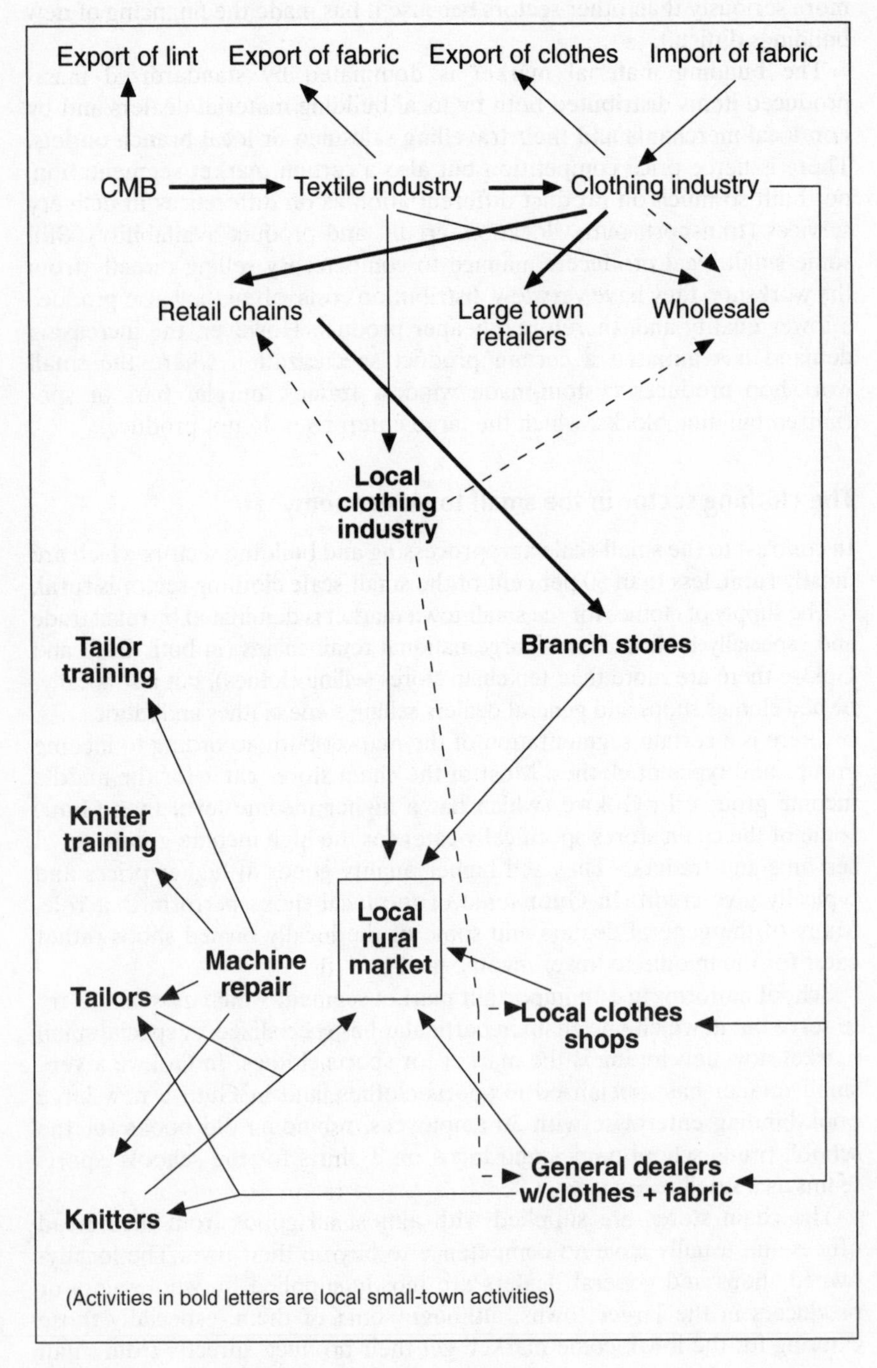

Figure 2.3 *The clothing industry and trade*

On the production side the clothing sector consists of knitters, tailors and a few larger enterprises which could be termed industrial. In Gutu there are three large clothes-making workshops with, respectively, five, fifteen to twenty and about thirty people employed. Their most important market is school uniforms, but the two largest are attempting to get into other markets as well. The largest, which at the time of our field work had only been in operation for eight weeks, had not yet developed a clear product specialization, but tried, apparently with some success, to produce women's dresses for the national retail chains, while the second largest has specialized in protective work clothes with company names printed on them for the non-local enterprise market. Both have had difficulties in getting into the local market, because the chain stores dominating it have no competence to buy locally. Both large enterprises have thus established their own retail outlets in Gutu centre and have salesmen travelling in the rural areas in order to get into the local market.

However, it has been necessary for both of them to go directly to the national market in order to get a sufficiently large market, where one has tried to sell to the large retail chains, the other to sell to the enterprise market.

The small tailors operating in the centres are mostly men[6] operating very small, mostly one-man, enterprises. Some of them have their own or part of a shop, while others are operated on rented shop verandas. They are mostly doing repair work, but some of them also produce school uniforms. There are about five of these small tailors in Gutu and Gokwe. The small tailors mostly have no apprentices (although some train their children or nephews), but one of them has six paying apprentices and operates a regular six-month training programme. In addition to the independent tailors, some of the local shops selling clothes employ a tailor who mostly fits industrially produced clothes to customer size.

The knitting enterprises which knit sweaters on knitting machines are small enterprises, all operated by women. The market for knitwear is highly seasonal, concentrated on the few winter months, and few of the women can afford to produce stock the rest of the year. In order to counteract the seasonality of the market, a few combine the knitting with dressmaking, but many take in two to six paying apprentices who are trained over a three-month period. Others also have a sewing machine and do some tailoring/dressmaking which is less seasonal.

In Gutu, many of the small knitting enterprises are run by the wives of the larger general dealers in the centre and operated on the shop premises.

In Gokwe, the small knitting enterprises are rather operated as independent businesses. One of the reasons for this appears to be that there is a large number of small shops for rent in Gokwe on both council and private premises. This has made it relatively easier for women to establish themselves in Gokwe than in Gutu, where such small premises for rent are scarce. The knitwear is mostly sold from the shop or through saleswomen travelling in the rural areas. Very few sell through other retailers or wholesalers.

In addition to the training in tailoring and knitting which takes place in the small production enterprises, there is, especially in Gutu and to a smaller extent in Gokwe, a number of enterprises offering training on a larger scale in dressmaking and knitting.[7] These training centres are all run by women, mostly as private enterprises, but some by NGOs or co-operatives.

In Gutu, there is one knitting school offering three-month courses in knitting for up to 45 trainees at a time and four dressmaking schools offering six-month courses in dressmaking with an opportunity for extension with another six months in design and patternmaking. In Gokwe there are only two centres offering similar dressmaking courses. There appear to be around 150 knitters and 300 dressmakers trained in Gutu, and 25–30 knitters and 40 dressmakers in Gokwe in a normal year.

Most of the trainees from these small training centres get jobs in small workshops, mostly in Harare, Bulawayo or the larger provincial towns, and apparently until recently with little difficulty. Very few start directly on their own, because it requires both experience and capital to invest in a sewing or knitting machine.

The large industrial enterprises say that they cannot use the trainees from the small training centres. They have their own internal training, and the trainees from the small training centres are, in general, not even qualified to start on that internal training. One of the problems is that the small training schools operate with old household sewing machines which are much slower than the large machines used in the industry.

The large enterprises recruit their workers from the smaller workshops and apparently have had no difficulty in getting qualified candidates, although the employment in the industry has been growing rapidly during the 1980s. This indicates that there is a career pattern where the trainees from the small training centres work some years in the small workshops. Some of them leave their job when they get married, some start on their own, and others advance to the better-paid jobs in the formal industry.[8]

Thus, although the large industry does not find the small training centres satisfactory, the centres seem to play an important role, not only in developing the small enterprise sector, but also in creating a recruiting basis for the large enterprises.

The latest addition to the clothing industrial complex in Gutu is a recently-established specialized sewing machine repair shop.

Structural adjustment and the process of rural commercialization and industrialization

In economies, such as that of Zimbabwe, where a large part of the population is still kept in a semi-subsistence economy at the same time as the formal trade and industry is highly concentrated both organizationally and geographically, rural industrialization must be a combined process of consolidation and concentration of rural small-scale activities on the one hand and decentralization of formal sector activities on the other. How such policies can be pursued varies from sector to sector, depending on the structure of the sector and the degree of concentration. This, however, is seldom mirrored in the industrialization and development policies.

The industrialization policies under the current wave of structural adjustment policies consist of three major elements:

- trade liberalization and devaluation;
- privatization policies and reduction of the public sector;
- deregulation and small enterprise development support.

Such policies have also been under way in Zimbabwe since 1990. Their introduction, however, has been very gradual. Deregulation and privatization policies have hardly begun, and even trade liberalization has only taken place to a limited extent. In addition the severe drought during 1992 has thrown Zimbabwe into an economic crisis and delayed the structural adjustment process. It is, therefore, very difficult to know whether the present economic crisis in Zimbabwe is caused by the drought or by the structural adjustment policies.

Still, on the basis of the three sector studies presented above, we shall in the following attempt to discuss the likely impact of the different structural adjustment policies.

Privatization policies and reduction of the public sector

One of the main arguments behind the structural adjustment policies has been that government controlled prices in many African countries have led to insufficient food production: because prices have been kept so low, it has not been attractive for farmers to produce food crops for the market. At the same time pan-territorial prices and politically-determined low consumer prices result in growing deficits and subsidies to the marketing boards. Therefore, it is argued, prices should be set free.

In Zimbabwe, however, this argument is only partly true. It is true that the controlled price on maize has been so low that the large commercial farmers have shifted away from maize to better-paying specialized crops for the growing urban market and especially for the export market. Trade liberalization measures which have permitted commercial farmers to keep some of the foreign currency they earn on export crops have furthered this shift away from maize.

On the other hand, the price level, together with improved agricultural infrastructure in the communal areas during the 1980s, have been sufficient to increase the marketed maize and cotton production in the communal areas from very little to more than half of the total marketed production. Although the agricultural production in the communal areas for climatic reasons tends to be rather unstable, this had, by the end of the 1980s, resulted in the production of a maize surplus and a large increase in the cotton production. However, it has also required increasing subsidies to the marketing boards.

Rather than support the agricultural production, the structural adjustment policies have, in their attempt to reduce the parastatal deficits, led to falling real producer prices since the end of the 1980s, closure of some of the rural depots, and sell-out of the food security stock. The result has been reduced incomes in the rural areas and growing food prices. This situation has of course been aggravated by the generally-increasing consumer prices due to devaluation and drought.

So far it is especially the low income and rural consumer markets which have contracted. Thus one of the largest garment retailers in the country operating two large retail chains, one for the upper income market and one for the low income and rural market, had in 1991 (basically before the drought) a large surplus in the chain catering for the high income market but a large deficit in the chain catering for the low income and rural markets.

As in other African countries, the privatization policies have been more concerned with the selling out of the agricultural marketing parastatals from the top rather than dismantling the large monopolies from the bottom. It might make more sense to keep the export/import functions and the responsibility for operating food security stocks in government hands, but decentralize and de-monopolize the domestic and especially the rural trade and processing activity which are areas in which both the parastatal and the large private semi-monopolistic enterprises are least efficient. This would benefit development in general and create a larger market for small and medium-sized enterprises.

In the grain sector one way of doing this would (as shown previously) be to liberalize the marketing board's selling price rather than its buying price. With such a policy it would still be attractive to grow and market food in the peripheral areas, but it would open up for a partial decentralization of the processing industry, and lead to reduced transport costs and small-scale industrialization in the small towns.

In the building sector, a decentralization of ministerial and parastatal building decisions to district or provincial level, together with changed tendering practices and increased local supervision, could lead to a gradual quantitative as well as qualitative improvement in the small-town building sector.

Just as the effect of privatization policies depends very much on the way they are carried out, so does the effect of retrenchment policies in the public sector. A retrenchment which does not lead to decentralization will hit the small towns and rural areas hard, partly because the civil servants here represent a large share of the local market, and partly because it will make it difficult to support and control development in the local private sector.

Trade liberalization policies and devaluation

Benefits from trade liberalization and devaluations in the short run primarily accrue to the larger enterprises operating on the import/export markets. In Zimbabwe this also comprises the large commercial farms, which as part of the liberalization policies have been allowed to retain part of the foreign currency they earn on export.

In most industries this direct benefit is likely to be highly concentrated, because it follows export. Thus in the clothing sector, only 25 large enterprises are responsible for almost all the export, while export in the building sector is minimal.

Trade liberalization may also benefit the small and medium-sized home market industries by improving their access to production inputs, machinery, and spare parts, albeit at increased prices. In connection with the structural adjustment policy the government has established the *Zimbabwe Investment Centre* as a 'single-window' focal point for processing of investment applications, which earlier had to pass through many different ministries (Republic of Zimbabwe, 1991). Some of the newly-established medium-sized enterprises in the towns appear to have benefited from this and obtained investment permission and foreign currency allocations very rapidly (six weeks). For other reasons it took, however, one to two years before they were actually established.

On the other hand it is still difficult for small enterprises without export earnings of their own to obtain imported production inputs, small machines, tools and spare parts.

Trade liberalization also leads to increased competition from imported goods and, therefore, hits enterprises operating on the home market. Of the three sectors we have studied this will especially hit the clothing sector. Some of the negative effects might be avoided by differentiated trade liberalization where only, or especially, the import of intermediate goods and machinery is liberalized. In Zimbabwe such a policy has been attempted and the import of clothing is therefore still limited. On the other hand, the clothing sector has not benefited from a liberalized import of intermediate goods, because its main input, fabric, is treated as a consumer good and still protected.

The result is that the Cotton Marketing Board and the textile mills are permitted to export the best quality cotton lint and fabric, while the clothing industry is forced to buy either lower quality domestically-produced fabric or very expensive imported fabric.

In total, the effect of the trade liberalization so far seems to be quite limited, and, especially for enterprises catering for the low income market, mostly negative because their market has contracted due to food price increases and devaluation.

In the longer run, one might of course hope that more enterprises will start to export and leave the home market to the smaller enterprises.

However, this will require an upgrading and increased product quality in the small and medium-sized enterprises, which with a strongly contracting home market is unlikely to happen.

Deregulation and small enterprise development support

Deregulation of licensing, local by-laws and building regulations etc., and direct support schemes for small or new enterprises, mostly providing management training and financial support, will primarily benefit the development of small enterprises. In both the building and clothing sectors, local differences in planning and administrative practices have had considerable impact on the development of small enterprises, and led to different developments in the studied towns.

The problem with deregulation policies and direct support schemes, which require government resources, detailed legislation and local initiatives, is that they take much longer to realize than trade liberalization and privatization from the top and are often counteracted by public sector retrenchment. Therefore, when the deregulation policies and small enterprise support schemes are introduced, the home market has already contracted, leaving little room for the development of new enterprises.

On the other hand, concurrent with the structural adjustment policy, there has been an increasing awareness of the need to develop a small enterprise sector. Especially since 1990 there has been a rapid change in attitude away from a narrow focus on large-scale industry toward a more balanced view. Government, donors, NGOs and banks have all become very active in setting up small enterprise support schemes. So far, however, the effect seems to have been quite limited and mostly concentrated in the largest towns. In the two district service centres very few activities have yet benefited from such schemes.

On the structure of markets

From the perspective of small-town studies presented in this paper one of the main problems with the industrialization policies derived from the structural adjustment paradigm is that they conceive of the enterprises, large or small, as operating in a large homogeneous and stable market rather than in the highly segmented and unstable market existing in reality.

The intention of the liberalization policies is, of course, to create that homogeneous stable market. However, even in the more open market, economies now developing in the industrial world are not characterized by homogeneous stable markets, but by increasing specialization, segmentation and instability due to rapid innovation and product specialization. Networking and flexible specialization as active enterprise strategies are precisely the response to these conditions.

Interestingly, the markets in developing countries are also characterized by segmentation and instability, although caused by extreme income differences, unstable and seasonal incomes, lack of infrastructure and unstable commodity supplies, rather than by innovation and product specialization. As in the developed countries, the response of the enterprises is networking and flexible specialization, but networking and specialization of a different kind than in the industrialized world. In order to withstand the large instability, small enterprises rely on family networks and hierarchical patron-client relationships, which may be highly exploitative, but give some guarantee for survival. Also, specialization and market segmentation are based on delivery services (transport, credit and commodity availability) rather than product specialization, although increasingly, this is also found.

In a modern world economy dominated by market segmentation and rapid change, there is little reason to believe that the segmented and unstable markets in the developing countries should turn homogeneous and stable as a result of structural adjustment policies. The more likely scenario is that they stay segmented and unstable, but for changing reasons, and hopefully on higher levels of productivity.

This, however, requires policy prescriptions based on assumptions about market segmentation rather than on the assumptions about homogeneous markets on which the structural adjustment policies are based. Trade liberalization, privatization and deregulation may well be the main ingredients of such policy prescriptions, but rather than focusing primarily on the export production, and assuming that the benefits will filter automatically to the other parts of the production system, they should give equal weight to increasing the productivity and production in large and small enterprises serving the urban and rural home markets.

The main argument for free trade in manufactured goods is that it allows for scale economies and, therefore, higher productivity (see Colclough, 1991). However, in developing countries where most production takes place in small enterprises, there is, even without free international trade, plenty of room for increased productivity both through consolidation of industries and exploitation of scale economies and through the development of flexible production and collective efficiency.

3 Gradual diffusion of flexible techniques in small and medium-size enterprise networks

ARNI SVERRISSON

In recent years, critical voices have increasingly been raised about the general orientation of prevailing industrialization policies in Africa. Several such writers have drawn upon discussions about flexible manufacturing, and the corollary criticism of 'mass-production' as the universal paradigm on industrial development, in order to substantiate their suggestions for alternative industrialization strategies (Smillie, 1991; Kaplinski, 1990).

In these writings about African industrialization problems, the 'flexible specialization' paradigm, the alternative to 'mass production' posited by Piore and Sabel in their 1984 book *The Second Industrial Divide*, has served as a point of departure rather than a paradigm in the proper sense, largely due to the special circumstances obtaining in Africa. The economic weakness of the indigenous petty bourgeoisie in most African countries, its lack of social cohesion and the absence of channels for an organized expression of its interests all make it difficult to apply the 'flexible specialization' thesis directly in Africa. Lastly, the strong role played hitherto by the state-based rentier technocracy (and its 'donor' counterparts) in formulating industrialization policies is largely specific to Africa, although similar phenomena have been observed elsewhere.

In what follows, technological networks and gradual mechanization in small and medium-sized carpentry enterprises in two secondary cities, Nakuru and Mutare, in Kenya and Zimbabwe respectively, are discussed on the basis of data collected in two field trips, in 1988 and 1990.

Technological networks are mainly of two kinds, integrated and flexible. Integrated technological networks are characterized by high interdependence of the parts, rigid relationships and a hierarchical distribution of power. Their establishment and growth calls for extensive control, even total subsumption, of the economic and social milieu in which they function, and implies radical technical change encompassing large sections of the society in question. Flexible technological networks are, by contrast, characterized by relative autonomy of the parts, volatile and changeable relationships, and a decentralized power distribution. They are not established, rather, new forms are generated and evolve continuously on the basis of preceding social and technical arrangements. This process, therefore, implies gradual technological change, the immediate impact of which may be confined to limited sections of the society concerned.

Further, enterprises or production units can be organized in a more or less flexible or integrated fashion, according to the character of their *internal* networks. Whole enterprise groups can also be organized either way, and it is therefore necessary to distinguish between these two levels of analysis. Any firm or group of firms under study can be placed along these dimensions, according to whether the firm itself is organized on a flexible basis or not and whether it belongs to a flexible or integrated network or not.

Flexible and integrated enterprises

Most small and medium-sized carpentry enterprises in Africa are good examples of flexible enterprises operating within flexible production networks. In such enterprises, a range of technological sophistication can be found, from the simplest handtools to next to complete collections of machines. For convenience, the enterprises can be classified into three categories, which in what follows will be called the low, intermediate and high sophistication groups, or groups I, II or III respectively. Enterprises in group I use only handtools, those in group two are partially mechanized, and in group III, the production process in the enterprises is next to completely mechanized. Most of them produce varied types of furniture, piece by piece, and design often varies with the wishes of the customers. Integrated furniture factories turning out standardized products in large batches are, in comparison, rare. Furthermore, the character of integration is social rather than technical in many cases. A production sequence is built up by combining several single-function machines of the type also seen in multipurpose production networks within flexible enterprises. These machines are used to cut and plane pieces of wood according to specifications given by the design of the final products, in large batches or continuously. The pieces are then brought to an assembly hall or area.

This type of production network can be contrasted with completely flexible mechanized networks, where a craftsman uses one machine after another in the process of shaping wood prior to assembly, which is then carried out by hand. This is the most common practice.

Another network type is where integration is more or less built into the hardware, and the range of potential output is therefore severely limited. One example of such production networks is the production of laminated pine bookshelves for export by an enterprise in Mutare. First, the pieces are planed to the right dimensions and then their ends are grooved in special machines, prior to the assembly of big laminated pieces of the same type as used for roofs in big buildings. These are then sawn to the desired dimensions, planed, profiled and sanded. The whole production line is arranged on the factory floor according to this particular sequence of production, in order to minimize transport, which is largely mechanical.

If we consider these different network types, it can be observed that production networks can be geared more or less permanently to a particular product. This can be achieved either by technical means, i.e. specialized machinery which can be used only for this product, or others closely related to it, or through reconfiguration of social relations in the workplace.

Permanently integrated networks which are built into the machinery used can be characterized as consisting of one central piece of machinery and ancillary machinery, the use of which is subservient to the central process. The sustainability of such paradigmatic 'mass production networks' depends on an ensemble of circumstances, such as a reliable supply of raw materials and the required inputs, including energy which in most cases means electricity. Further, specialized skills are often needed to supervise the network and maintain it, whereas the skills of the operators are less important. Varied machine parts which must be replaced or maintained regularly, such as cutting tools, must be readily available, as well as other spares, without which the whole production line will come to a standstill. Finally, demand for the product must be ensured, not only on the basis of general needs assessment, but actively, through the construction of a distribution system, by advertising and other manipulation of consumer tastes, etc. That this catalogue strongly resembles a list of troubles common to technology transfer projects is, of course, not a coincidence.

The primary *social* means of integrating the technological network within the enterprise is division of labour, or the allocation of specialized tasks to workers within the factory or workshop. The unity of the production process is in this case not ensured by the matching of machines and machine components, but by subdividing the process into several sequential or parallel parts, and allocating each to a worker or a number of workers. In carrying out their tasks, they use one or more machines or handtools, in the use of which they may become accomplished experts.

This type of organization prevailed in the three technologically most advanced furniture-producing enterprises studied in Mutare. Using multipurpose machinery, that is machines which could be used to produce a relatively wide range of products, and combining the work of the labourers through division of labour, these enterprises were able to solve some of the problems not so easily overcome in technically integrated production systems. Their product range was wide, and widening in the most advanced enterprise which was increasingly moving into customized production. They were therefore not dependent on the demand for one particular product, but could adapt their operations to external circumstances, over which they had, at any rate, little control. Similarly, restricted supplies of a particular input, such as formica, door hinges or plywood was a nuisance, but not a catastrophe, as production could temporarily be focused on products for which such inputs are not necessary.

The workers have, in these enterprises, become a cog in a 'machine', but this machine is not a mechanical construct. It is a social construct, the result of a particular form of organization, which included the combination of several machines. There is no technical imperative to organize the use of these machines in this particular way. Rather, it represents an effort to effectively control production and minimize the need for skilled workers. Another possible interpretation is that this type of organization is a cultural construct, i.e. it represents the right thing to do, emulating western enterprises without having the corresponding specialized machinery, or for that matter, needing it.

The mode of production organization described in the last paragraph can be contrasted with the most sophisticated furniture manufacturers in Nakuru. There, a foreman or the proprietor would ask a worker to make a particular piece, such as a dining-room table, and he would then make each part and join them, using each machine in turn, and finally, be paid for the whole piece. This type of network can therefore be characterized as mechanized craft-organized production. In this case, most workers have to be broadly skilled, and the room for participation by unskilled and semiskilled workers is limited.

Considering that the machines used in Nakuru and Mutare were quite similar, this contrast signifies clearly that technical change does not merely involve choices about types of equipment or techniques, but also, and separately, choices about the organization of production. The decline in the skills used at work which has been adjacent upon industrial development in Europe and the USA has not depended on mechanization *per se*, but rather on the introduction of 'mass-production' organization, and the concomitant sub-division of production tasks.

Neither the semi-flexible, socially-integrated network nor the truly flexible, mechanized craft-production network are completely free from the problems of mechanization. As in any mechanized activity, maintenance must be ensured. However, because the kind of machinery used is not specialized, it is also relatively widely available, and barring import restrictions, which was in fact quite a problem in Zimbabwe, they can be replaced. Further, the components of this kind of machinery are, with the exception of the cutting tools themselves, of the kind that can be found in any type of machinery, such as bearings of standardized sizes and electrical motors. Other components such as axles and pulleys can be produced or adapted without undue complications by local workshops.

When breakdowns occur, therefore, the consequences are limited in comparison with what happens in a technically integrated production network. To some extent, one machine can replace another. Simple grooves, for example, can be cut by a bench saw, if no rout is available. The bench saw can also double for the cross-cut saw, the planer for the thicknesser, and so on, if this is unavoidable. However, this implies that exact standards are not imposed by authorities or customers, and such is the case in the African furniture sector.

Further, most of the single function machines represent mechanization of an operation otherwise carried out by handtools. Hence, if one particular machine breaks down, this phase can be carried out temporarily by hand, or by hand-held powertools, which many enterprises 'keep in reserve' as it were, until the machine is repaired, without catastrophic losses in overall labour productivity. Where labour is cheap, the loss in capital productivity is even less pronounced.

It is this characteristic of flexible, mechanized production networks which is utilized by the intermediate group of carpentry enterprises in Nakuru and Mutare. These enterprises are *partially mechanized*, that is, one or more basic machines have been acquired, in a gradual fashion, acquiring one machine first, then the next and so on. The steps in the production process for which a machine is not available within the enterprise are either carried out with the use of handtools or subcontracted to a nearby colleague, who has the 'missing' machine. The latter is common in the case of turning, where no direct handtool substitute is available, but other functions can and are also organized in this way. Some of this machine work, such as preliminary sawing and planing, can also be carried out by timber merchants.

The most commonly-found machine in Nakuru is the woodlathe, after which comes the bench saw or re-saw. The bench saw was, however, the machine most frequently found in Mutare. In second place there, and third in Nakuru, was the hand-held electric drill, which is mainly used to speed up the cutting of mortises.

In view of the versatility of the bench saw, it is no surprise that this machine is the first choice of many carpenters entering on a graduation path through gradual mechanization. Other fairly common machines in both countries were planers, thicknessers, band-saws and cross-cut saws. Not so common tools were sanding devices, routs and mortise cutters, tenon cutters and pneumatic varnishing equipment. Multiple tool machines were rare, and the only types found were fourcutters and planers combined with thicknessers.

This type of machine, and in particular so-called combined machines, in which several tools are powered by a single motor, would no doubt be the most appropriate technically speaking both because of their flexibility, and because electrical motors are difficult to acquire and maintain and an expensive component of any machine. The labour organization and skill of workers in most enterprises should also facilitate the diffusion of this kind of machine. However, due to the gradual character of mechanization in most enterprises and the role of secondhand markets, reconditioned machines and local assembly of machines, combined machines are rarely found.

Flexible enterprise networks

Just as production networks internal to enterprises can be more or less flexible, enterprise networks can also be analysed from this point of view.

An enterprise network is here taken to include a group of enterprises which produces the same, similar or substitutable products, and the upstream and downstream linkages of this group. Furthermore, other types of relations, such as created by circulation of the labour force, interpersonal and other communication channels, credit, relations with government agencies, and so on, are important aspects of the network. An overview of this approach is provided in Figure 3.1.

An extreme case of integrated and flexible networks co-existing with minimal interconnections, is described by Bagachwa in his study of grain milling in Tanzania (1992). On the one hand, through the National Milling Corporation, the government attempted to create an integrated system for the production of maize and rice flour. This operation was sustained by the regulation of the grain trade, a legal monopoly on purchases, an elaborate distribution system, a transport system, and so on. Side by side with this

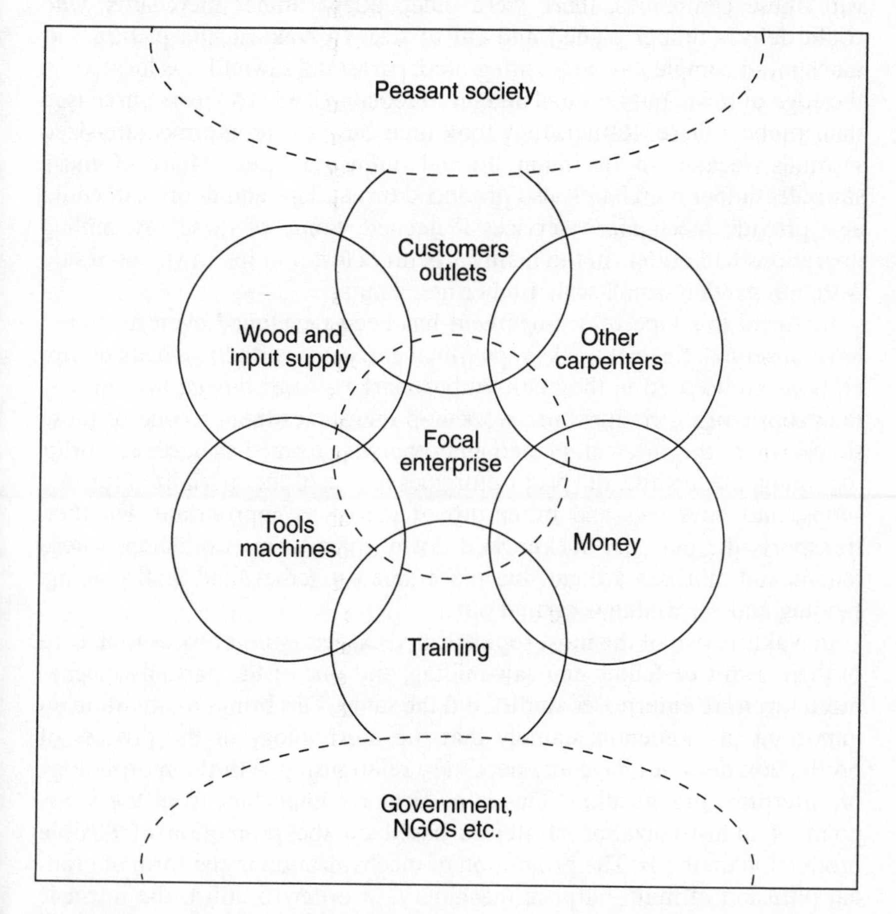

Figure 3.1 *An overview of carpentry networks in Mutare and Nakuru*

nationwide network, local mills operating on a service basis, that is, milling flour brought by customers, and household milling continued to exist. This extreme situation was untypical, however, and could only survive in a politically regulated economy. When restrictions on the grain trade were lifted, private commercial grain mills immediately emerged.

More common are networks which link together enterprises of different types, that is combine both flexibly organized and integrated enterprises simultaneously, as well as including enterprises with different degrees of technological sophistication. This is how the wood-working industry in Nakuru and Mutare is organized.

Let us first consider the 'upstream' section of the carpentry networks in the two towns. In Mutare the provision of timber was completely dominated by two forest and wood-processing companies, one of which was a parastatal, and the other a subsidiary of a multinational corporation. Along with these companies, there were independent timber merchants, who could deliver timber planed and cut to size. In Nakuru, the picture was much more complex. A large, integrated, parastatal sawmill was located on the edge of town, but no small and intermediate-sized producers purchased their timbers there. Rather, they took their business to intermediate-sized sawmills, located in the main 'formal' industrial area. Many of these sawmills/timber merchants also produced turned legs and doors and could also provide mechanized services if needed. Some of these saw-milling operations had outlets in the main carpentry cluster in the town, alongside with independent small-scale timber merchants.

In Accra this type of arrangement has been developed even further, I have observed. Special workshops which carry out varied mechanized operations are located in the main timber market. After buying his timbers, the proprietor of the furniture workshop then takes them to one of these shops, where they are cut, planed and otherwise formed as necessary prior to joining. Meanwhile, the proprietor goes to one of the specialized turning shops, and buys legs and other turned pieces as appropriate. He then transports the material in 'knocked down' form to his workshop, where tenons and mortises are cut, the piece glued together, and final planing, sanding and varnishing is carried out.

In Nakuru, two of the most sophisticated carpentry enterprises took care of their own tree-felling and saw-milling, and one of the partially mechanized furniture enterprises studied did the same. This brings to attention an important phenomenon, namely that the morphology of the process of production does not have any necessary relationship with the morphology of enterprise organization. This is particularly important from the viewpoint of industrialization strategies based on the promotion of flexible production methods. The promotion of mechanization in the form of gradual diffusion of multi-purpose machinery, in order to utilize the intrinsic flexibility of existing local production networks, does not call for neither a fixation on a particular size range, nor does it imply that a particular form of the social division of labour is preferred, such as craft-based organization.

Turning to the 'downstream' section of the woodworking networks in Nakuru and Mutare, the picture is quite different. In both towns, furniture is sold to customers through two distinct channels. One channel is mainstreet furniture shops, which are supplied by furniture workshops and factories in other towns. The other channel is sales directly from the workshops, or in exceptional cases, from small furniture shops located in the main carpentry areas within the town. Indeed, the premises of most workshops serve a double function, in that both the production of furniture and negotiations with customers are carried out in the same place.

This is reflected in the spatial structure of these workshops in Nakuru: work is usually carried out in a back room, or under a shed behind the building proper. Furniture is displayed in a front room and in front of the workshop. The shop attendant may be occupied with finishing work when there are no customers around, but the joining itself is usually carried out behind.

In Mutare, furniture was also displayed in front of the workshop, but work was also carried out in full view of prospective customers. Most of the workshops lacked backdoors, which are necessary for the typical Nakuru arrangement to develop. This added to the dualistic character of the Mutare furniture sector in that the 'informality' of the small-scale enterprises was obvious to the most casual observer, and provided a stark contrast to the cool and spacious showrooms of the mainstreet shops.

Quality differences are manifested to the customers at their contact points with the carpentry network, so the appearance of this point is by no means unimportant. However, the quality itself of the furniture pieces displayed in the carpentry workshops in Mutare also differed in most cases markedly from those available in the mainstreet shops. The reason for this is that good quality of handmade furniture, including such aspects as exactly cut joints, well-planed and sanded surfaces, etc., implies extra labour for which poor customers are not ready to pay. Rich customers, in turn, generally go to mainstreet shops where mechanically produced, cash-and-carry furniture is available, rather than engaging in the process of contracting a small-scale carpenter to make the desired piece.

In Nakuru, although the 'informal' character of most small-sized workshops was unmistakable, it was by no means as pronounced as in Mutare. Further, the actual quality of the furniture produced generally approached the standards of the mainstreet shops, and surpassed it in many cases. With his wife, one carpenter in Nakuru had in fact established a furniture shop in the local shopping area, where nice furniture was displayed and sold to well-off customers.

This had not, however, led to sales by small-scale carpenters to mainstreet furniture shops except occasionally. One such shop was owned by a family which also ran its own, flexibly organized, workshop. Otherwise, almost all the furniture sold came from the outside. The immediate reason for this was that the prices offered by mainstreet shops were too low in the view of those carpenters who had entered into at least preliminary negotiations. To put it otherwise: spending time negotiating prices with customers in the workshop paid better than supplying mainstreet shops and leaving this task to them. In this case, specialization is not advantageous.

A similar dualism as appears in the sales phase could be observed in matters of credit and provision of working capital. The most sophisticated carpentry enterprises in both countries had regular relationships with banks and other savings and credit institutions, and could when need arose supplement their own working capital from these sources. The handtool-based enterprises, as well as most of the partially mechanized enterprises, relied almost exclusively on customers' deposits and own funds for working capital. This is undoubtedly one of the explanations of the gradual character of mechanization in these enterprises, as well as the gradual build-up of a collection of handtools in those enterprises which had not reached the point of mechanization. However, it also follows that credit on a large scale is not quite as salient from the viewpoint of a gradual diffusion strategy, as it is when technical change is expected to progress, if at all, by leaps and bounds.

Machine networks and skills development

A stylized picture of the tool and machine aspects of the carpentry networks in Mutare and Nakuru is shown in Figure 3.2. First, let us note that in the focal enterprise there is a lathe. However, in the three other small carpentry enterprises shown (in practice there are many others) there are no lathes. In one of them, a planer is located, in another one, there is a saw, whereas in the third one, there is no machine. Hence, it is possible, and sometimes practised, that the planer owner planes for the lathe-owner and vice versa. More frequent, however, is the situation that obtains between the lathe-owner and the proprietor of the workshop with no machines. The machineless proprietor provides material to the lathe-owner, who then gives the work to one of his workers or does it himself, and charges a small sum for the favour.

However, in the figure, three additional lathe owners are shown. One is the lumberyard or timber merchant, as they are also called. The fact that vendors of timber often own lathes (and various other woodworking machines as well) is important. Most carpenters have to procure their materials in such a place, and hence, for the sake of convenience, may buy ready-made turned pieces (bed legs, table legs of different lengths etc.) or order legs according to specifications agreed upon with their customers. The third lathe shown is located in a specialized lathe shop, which concen-

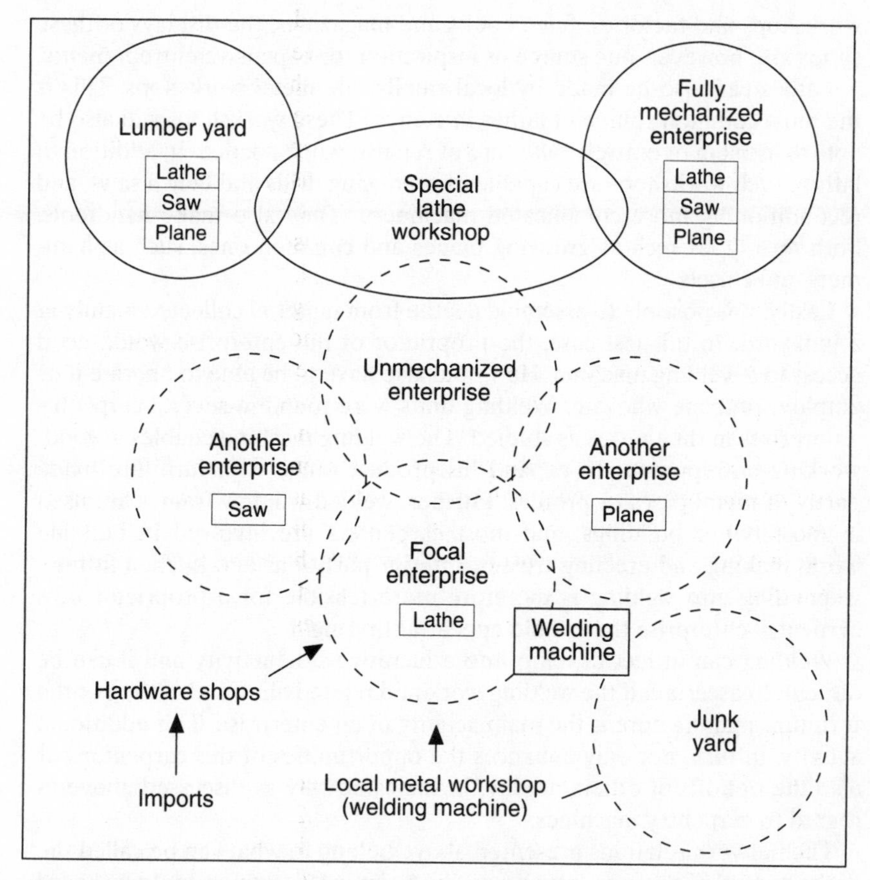

Figure 3.2 *Tool and machine aspects of carpentry networks*

trates on turning. The competitive strategy of such latheshops, as observed in Kenya, is to be located in the middle of a cluster of carpentry enterprises without lathes. The fourth lathe shown is located in a fully-mechanized workshop. This workshop does not have to rely on other enterprises for any mechanized services, but can provide them to others. This was rare, however. Most of the almost completely mechanized workshops were largely outside the realm of co-operative enterprise relationships. From this description we can see that a carpenter without a lathe has in this instance three or even four options as to where to get this turning done.

Continuing with the lathe, it is of interest to consider where it came from. One source is beyond the horizon of the network as it is presented here. This is when a machine is bought second hand for example at an auction occasioned by a bankruptcy. In addition, machines can be bought at better supplied hardware stores, but seldom are. Along with mechanized workshops and factories, fairs, books and magazines, the displays of these shops are, however, one source of inspiration for expansive entrepreneurs.

Lathes can also be made by local small-scale metal workshops. This is the most common source of lathes in Kenya. These workshops will also be able to assist in or entirely take care of repairs, when needed. In addition to lathes, such workshops are capable of producing drills and bench saws, and reconditioning more complicated machinery. They also make handtools, both rare types such as grooving planes and common ones, such as hammers and chisels.

Lastly, it is possible to assemble a lathe from material collected mainly at a junkyard. In this last case, the proprietor of the enterprise would need access to a welding machine. He would also have to be able to operate it or employ someone who can. Welding units were found in several carpentry enterprises in the two areas studied. The welding machine enables a woodworking entrepreneur to expand his product range with furniture made partly of metal pipes or profiles. Further, welded window frames are used in most better buildings, and most carpenters are involved in building work, making and erecting trusses, interior partitions and kitchen fittings. Expanding into welding is therefore more feasible for a proprietor of a carpentry enterprise that would appear at first sight.

Welding can in fact develop into a lucrative side activity and it can be difficult to ascertain if the welding work and related filing and cutting or the furniture manufacture is the main activity of an enterprise. This additional activity, in turn, not only enhances the opportunities of this carpenter but also the options of others nearby, in the same way as discussed above in regard to carpentry machines.

The network relations presented above belong to what can be called the 'lathe aspect' of the carpentry network. A similar discussion could be based on the relations surrounding planes or saws. They can be found in some but not all carpentry enterprises, and their existence in one enterprise increases the options of all carpenters in the vicinity. A parallel argument can also be developed with respect to certain advanced handtools, which were found in some but not all enterprises, such as saw-sets, grooving planes and rebate planes. Carpenters without these tools were able to borrow them from better-equipped colleagues.

Conclusion

It was noted above in the discussion of the 'upstream' side of carpentry networks, that there is no necessary correspondence between enterprise structure and the technologically-determined steps in the production process. This applies more or less to any collection of techniques which are combined in a social network, due to the fact that they can be integrated in any way which is technically and socially feasible. One consequence of this the possibility of gradual diffusion of mechanized techniques and the different forms and degrees of 'vertical integration' discussed above.

Furthermore, in both cases development through step-wise expansion of the confines of an existing complex of production arrangements plays an important role. In retrospect, it is easy to see why this is the case. Generally, people are more likely to extend, modify and improve what they already have than embark upon totally different ways of production. This latter possibility, which sometimes is taken to be the paradigmatic mode of development, can only arise, thrive and prosper in late-industrializing countries in special circumstances. Substantial capital infusion from the outside, and the provision of adequate infrastructure, as well as a preferential government policy, are all needed if such a strategy is to succeed. This is not enough, however. As radically new social arrangements are called for to make the new technology viable, its diffusion depends on this social process rather than technical efficiency or economic competitiveness in the strict sense. Such radical change in the entire social fabric is difficult to 'engineer' from above.

The gradual mode of diffusion is also reinforced by the relatively low concentration of accumulated capital achieved within most flexible networks and the preference of banks (and 'donors') for large-scale, integrated projects, which leads to further scarcity of capital in small and intermediate-sized enterprises. Volatile demand also reinforces this trend.

From this follows that the issue of technical change can be linked to issues of the 'new' comparative political economy of development. This approach contends that there is not one general path to development, but multiple paths, the features of which can be fruitfully compared (Evans and Stephens, 1988; Mouzelis, 1988). Such paths are partly moulded by historical contingencies, which elude attempts at generalization. However, it is possible to indicate, at least at a general level, common features or patterns, which can be expected to be replicated in most cases. Such patterns, or analogous processes, can then be used to guide research (Stinchcombe, 1978). The role of resilient and resistant social complexes, the appearance of technological disjunctions, the formation of coexisting and competing technological complexes, constituted by typical technologies and the social relations sustaining them, are among the phenomena which it is fruitful to study comparatively.

In conclusion, what can be seen at work in the carpentry collectives in Mutare and Nakuru is a different type of industrialization logic than implied by conceptions which assume linear development towards ever-increasing scale of production within an enterprise. This type of mechanization may not be a strategic alternative all on its own, but it represents an alternative industrialization model, which can and does coexist with the traditional model of industrialization.

In this type of networks, techniques diffuse according to criteria different from those assumed by the traditional diffusion model, in which efficient techniques take over from inefficient techniques as soon as the risk of adoption becomes reasonable and the cost of the new technique has become comparable to the cost of the old one. Rather, the efficient technique, in this instance, only diffuses in so far as flexibility can be maintained, and labour organization can remain basically unchanged.

4 New competition and flexible specialization in Indonesia and Burkina Faso

MEINE PIETER VAN DIJK

Empirical material collected in Indonesia (Van Dijk and Kameo, 1991) and in Burkina Faso (Van Dijk, 1991) will be used to demonstrate the usefulness of concepts such as flexible specialization and the new competition to understand the dynamics of the industrial sector in these two developing countries. At the end of the paper some conclusions will be drawn concerning the implications of these new approaches for the theory of industrialization and for the formulation of industrialization strategies.

Theoretical framework

The attractiveness of the structure–conduct–performance theory is that regressions can be carried out taking some indicator of performance as the variable to be explained.[1] Market concentration (measured for example by a Herfindahl index) and expenditures on research and development are often used as explanatory variables in the SCP model. However, the concepts of flexible specialization and the new competition suggest the use of indicators to assess the empirical relevance of flexible specialization and the new competition as well.[2] We will develop and use such indicators in this contribution.

The theory of the firm is a standard part of microeconomic theory. Empirical applications have often taken the form of estimating production functions, taking a black-box approach. Recently, analytical models have been developed, going beyond the black-box conception of a production function, searching for a deeper understanding, based on a contractual view.[3] In their review article of the theory of the firm Holmstrom and Tirole (1989) focus on the limits and the nature of the firm, the financing of firms, the role of management and the internal organization of the firm, and conclude that it is necessary to increase the evidence/theory ratio. A limit on research at the firm level is not enough, however, to understand the dynamics of the industrial sector in developing countries. We will argue that industry-level variables, as well as national and international variables, need to be taken into account.

Piore and Sabel (1984) argue that the history of industrialization has held open one major alternative to the system of mass production, namely craft production, based on the flexible use of general-purpose machinery by skilled workers capable of manufacturing a wide range of products for constantly changing markets. This idea is substantiated by evidence from Japan, Germany and Italy.

Flexible specialization and microenterprise development can be related in various different ways. Mendez-Rivero (1991) mentions that in Venezuela the growth of microenterprises between 1980 and 1988 was part of 'a strategy of cost flexibilization engaged in by larger enterprises'. This consisted of transferring the cost of an erratic demand to them. He concluded that informalization of the labour force is one of the ways in which the burden of the labour market regulations could be bypassed by these larger enterprises.[4] Piore and Sabel also stress the importance of subcontracting, clustering and networking which may imply relations between small firms (the small-scale variant of flexible specialization), or between small and big firms (the large-scale variant) and those variables will also be taken into account.

Best (1990) introduced the new competition concept, pointing at the industrial successes of the newly industrializing countries (NICs) and Japan compared with the lack of such success in the United Kingdom and the United States. Best stresses the importance for industrial development of different modes of organization, of an export-orientation, of flexibility and of conquering niche markets. His arguments are:

1. In the United States the problem of industrial decline is posed in terms of productivity instead of in organizational terms (p.3).
2. The United Kingdom and United States focused on demand management, not on supply, 'to regulate demand for purposes of stabilization policy' (p.200).
3. The easy explanations of the failure to compete, such as the high unit-labour costs, the heavy government regulation or the size of the public sector, can be contradicted by pointing to the higher unit-labour costs in Germany, the fact that Japanese firms are even more regulated and the bigger size of the public sector in Sweden (p.6).

An advantage of the approach of Piore and Sabel is that they mention a number of relevant variables and specify the relations between them. As such the concept of flexible specialization is somewhat easier to operationalize than the new competition concept. On the other hand, flexible specialization does not take into account the broader context of relevant developments in the world economy, which Best (1990) stresses so much. Another disadvantage of the approach of Piore and Sabel is that they suggest that there are only two possible types of production systems: mass production or flexible specialization. For this reason, Best considers flexible specialization to be a dynamic version of Marshall's industrial district, namely a particular strategy for competitive success that is open to groups of small firms. His definition of an innovation is also broader and he points at a process of vertical disintegration which he considers part and parcel of the new competition (also see Van Dijk *et al.*, 1992).

Methodology to determine the dynamics of the industrial sector

The research in Indonesia and Burkina Faso focused on the actual and potential development of the industrial sector and on which factors determine the dynamics of industrial firms (small, medium and large) in these countries. Data collection and analysis focused variables identified in Table 4.1. Particular attention was given to the importance of clustering of micro and small enterprises for forward and backward linkages and to the importance of networks in the exchange of information and diffusion innovation. The networks of micro and small enterprises also include their external relations. Where do they buy raw materials, tools and spare parts? What are the sources of credit, and new ideas concerning the organization of the production? What is the technology used, and how do they improve the quality of their products? Are there subcontracting relations; and which marketing channels have been developed?

Table 4.1 gives the operationalization of the two concepts used. Some of the variables concerning the firm level in this table require judgement. A classification of enterprises as following the flexible specialization or new competition approach made on the basis of our survey in Burkina Faso

Table 4.1 Operationalization in Indonesia and Burkina Faso

Developments in world economy:
- existence of possible export markets;
- no protection of these markets;
- no production or marketing monopolies;
- growth of world economy;
- segmentation of markets;
- available capital and technologies.

National or macro-level indicators:
- share industrial sector in Gross Domestic Product (GDP)
- growth of industrial sector
- export performance (growth export manufactured goods
- liberalization investment regime and financial markets

Firm-level indicators:

Variable	*Flexible specialization*	*The new competition*
Technology	Multi-purpose/skilled	Flexible/variable
Innovation	In product and process	Financial/marketing
Interfirm co-operation	Subcontracting	All kinds of arrangements
	Clustering	Vertical disintegration
	Networking	Export-orientation
	Skilled labour force	Segmented markets

may consequently be somewhat subjective. Variables which were not included because they are difficult to measure in a survey are innovative mentality and collective efficiency.

We did classify the formal sector industrial enterprises in Burkina Faso on the basis of their technology and innovations, the interfirm relations, and the importance of clusters and networks, and skilled labour. For flexible specialization clustering, networks and the presence of skilled labour were the specific variables; while for the new competition the existence of export orientation, catering for segmented markets and vertical disintegration were also taken into consideration. The score for each firm was based on at least one point for technology or innovation (if these were important), and one point for the other characteristics mentioned in Table 4.1 under firm level indicators (if they applied). If the total score was at least three we considered that the enterprise followed the flexible specialization and/or the new competition approach. Five could be classified as following both approaches, while three followed specifically the flexible specialization and three other as following the new competition approach.

The evidence in Indonesia and Burkina Faso

The two countries are quite different and were taken because we happened to do research in these countries.[5] They are, however, somewhat representative of Asia and Africa. Indonesia can be seen as representative of the kind of industrial development taking place in South East Asia, which could be called the spreading of the NICs model. Burkina Faso is quite typical of the slow (industrial) development taking place in many African countries. Both countries are going through a process of structural adjustment, which implies a change of economic policies. In Indonesia this process was triggered off by the low oil price in 1982, which forced the government to attract foreign capital by liberalizing the capital market and boosting the export of non-oil products. In Burkina Faso the adjustment was necessary after a period of overspending by the government and too tight control on the economy (1982–87) resulting in a decline of economic growth. It boils down to a transition from a government-controlled to a market-oriented economy.

Table 4.2 compares Indonesia and Burkina Faso as far as the macro level indicators are concerned. In the framework of this paper we will not discuss the developments in the world economy mentioned in Table 4.1. Table 4.2 shows Indonesia is much further on as far as industrialization is concerned. The share of the sector in the Gross Domestic Product (GDP) is substantially higher, the growth of the sector is faster, and the share of industrial products in exports is more important than in the case of Burkina Faso. Indonesia is paving its way to become an industrialized nation at the turn of the century (*Indonesia Magazine*, Jan.–Feb. 1991).[6] The country has been

Table 4.2 Macro level indicators Indonesia and Burkina Faso

Indicator	Indonesia	Burkina Faso
Population (millions 1989)	178.2	8.8
Per capita GDP (US dollars 1989)	500	330
Industrial sector share in GDP 1989	37%	26%
Manufacturing sector share in GDP 1989	17%	15%
Growth of industrial sector 1980–89	5.3%	3.9%
Growth of manufacturing sector 1980–89	12.7%	2.4%
Export manufactured goods, 1989	32%	11%
Liberalization investment regime	1982	–
Liberalization of financial markets	1982	–

Source: World Bank (1991).

very successful in boosting its exports of manufactured goods, but still feels the need to further enhance the exports of manufactured goods. Certain provinces are hardly benefiting, however, particularly the outer islands. In the non-oil sector, West Java, East Java and Jakarta are the most important industrial centres, with two-thirds of the production of the medium and large-scale industries in 1985. Central Java's share is surprisingly small.

Industrialization in Indonesia

The industrial structure in Indonesia used to be dominated by resource-based industries; industries catering for a population with a low level of per capita income. The small share of capital industries in the industrial sector of Indonesia is striking. In the category of medium and large industries, labour-intensive textiles, food products, tobacco and wood-processing industries dominate. The transition process had a number of characteristics.

The major dimension of Indonesia's industrial transformation lies in its rapid diversification, according to Hill (1990). There are many rapidly-growing industries, most of which are capital intensive. The very small ones are excluded from this dynamic development, however. The role of cottage industries (less than five employees) declined, while that of small-scale enterprises (between five and twenty employees) doubled between 1975 and 1986. Hill further notes a consistent trend of growing employment and productivity among the large and small industries. The differentiation between the large and small ones in terms of markets, technology, and labour may explain the impressive performance of each of these two categories.

Indonesia has faced the development of a stronger indigenous industrial base in the eighties, although there is still the question what has happened outside Java. The industrial structure changed considerably and there is a trend to more capital and skill-intensive industries. The industrial sector is working at a larger scale and has vastly increased its range of products.

Productivity and real wages have increased substantially, although there are still important inter-industry productivity differentials. Indonesia will have a problem of a shortage of skilled workers, necessary for the next step in the industrialization process: the move from simple labour-intensive to more sophisticated industries. The future for Indonesia's export of industrial products will depend on a number of developments in the world economy. What will be the effects of the changes which took place in Europe in 1992?[7] What will happen in the rest of the world?[8]

A few things are important for Indonesia's industrial development. The country has to continue to increase its exports and to keep an export-market orientation. To achieve this it will be necessary to assure the necessary supply of capital and technology. Finally the development of intrasectoral linkages is very important and the subcontracting system which is actually encouraged will need to be promoted in a more systematic way. Inspired by the Japanese and forced by the economic crisis triggered off by decreasing oil revenues in the early eighties, Indonesia has embarked upon industrial policies that created the conditions for industrial development according to flexible specialization and the new competition.

The industrial sector of Burkina Faso

In Burkina Faso the industrial sector is not yet that important. Its growth and the growth of exports of industrial products are not yet as high as in Indonesia, although the figures in Table 4.2 show an increase in the share of the manufacturing sector in GDP (from 11 per cent in 1965 to 17 per cent in 1989) and a substantial increase in the exports of manufactured products (from 5 to 11 per cent between 1965 and 1989). We did identify an important role for small and medium enterprises in the industrialization process, and the advantages of being located in a cluster came out very clearly (Van Dijk, 1992b).

At this stage of development, for the very small micro and small enterprises that make up the informal sector in Burkina, flexible specialization is not yet the strategy which helps them to survive (Van Dijk, 1992b). More traditional mechanisms are used. Innovations, clustering, subcontracting and entrepreneurship are not yet the key characteristics of a dynamic informal sector entrepreneur. Instead, personal relations, a good location, the choice of a promising activity and a number of economic variables such as initial investments and the chosen technology are more important for success. Government policies have also not yet been very favourable towards this type of development.

The situation in the modern industrial sector, however, is different from the informal sector. The lack of industrial protection in the eighties, because of lacking government funds, has increased the competition between enterprises of different sizes. The suspension of the investment code has also taken away the positive bias towards medium and large-scale industrial enterprises, and has given the small enterprises a better chance to compete.

The number of modern industrial establishments increased about 25 per cent between 1980 and 1991. In 1980 there were an estimated 120 modern industrial enterprises, and in 1991 information was collected concerning some 150 different industrial enterprises. There may even be more modern enterprises, given the somewhat fluid distinction between industries and some trading companies (e.g. in the leather, and fruit and vegetables sector) and the diffuse demarcation line between the informal and the industrial sector.

The modern industrial sector is dynamic in terms of number of new entrants and the number of enterprises that have disappeared. One-quarter of the modern sector industrial enterprises studied in 1991 had started or restarted during the last two years. Almost one-fifth of these enterprises (18 per cent) were not operating, either because of a 'chomage technique' or because the firm went bankrupt. At least five enterprises in the sample need to be reorganized to become profitable. Another five enterprises are waiting to be privatized, while others are looking for foreign partners, often not knowing how to start.

Exits and entries in the modern industrial sector are very common. Consequently, the number of modern industrial establishments increased substantially between 1981 and 1991. In 1981 there were about 126 modern industrial enterprises (Van Dijk, 1990). The Census of Commercial and Industrial Activities (1988) provides details concerning 147 different industrial enterprises. In the mid-eighties, one-third of the industrial enterprises (42) stopped activity (UNIDO, 1985). If 147 were counted in 1991, this means 63 industries started or restarted their activities during the last five years.

Another trend that can be detected is an increase in government participation in the capital of industrial enterprises in the eighties and a subsequent decrease in the nineties. Foreign capital has declined during the same period. The formal sector industries often required much protection and subsidies, but had limited impact in terms of employment or relations with other firms. UNIDO estimated total employment in the manufacturing sector in 1985 to be 8500 and this figure has not changed very much according to the present survey, because of reorganizations of existing firms and new firms starting with limited number of employees. The same UNIDO report notes the low degree of capacity utilization (50 per cent at the average in 1985) and the lack of integration, particularly of the larger industries. The latter has somewhat improved according to the survey.

The Sankara Government was less generous with tax concessions than its predecessors. This was reflected in the 1984 Investment code, which was favourable to private and foreign investment, but was intended to make the transition from special regimes to common rule easier and to increase the amount of tax to be collected from the industrial sector. Most industries were no longer protected by the *Code des investissements* at the end of the eighties. Nor does the government manage any longer to close the borders for competing industrial products. These developments have contributed to the bankruptcy or interruption of production in at least 29 cases, and have contributed to operating losses in another 19 cases.

In 1992 a number of industries were starting to expand production again in response to the opportunities provided by the new government and the structural adjustment programme. Table 4.3 gives the averages for the sample of 55 modern sector industrial enterprises, divided into six subsectors: agroprocessing, textile, leather, metal, woodworking and chemical industries. A detailed description of the subsectors can be found in a report prepared for the World Bank (Van Dijk, 1992b).

Flexible specialization in Burkina Faso's modern industrial sector

Five of the 55 enterprises interviewed could be classified as fitting both in the flexible specialization and in the new competition approach. Another three were classified as following a flexible specialization approach and three more as showing to opt for the new competition. Typical examples of flexible specialization enterprises could be found in the metal and woodworking sectors, and also in fruit and vegetable processing.

Entrepreneurs opting for these approaches are private entrepreneurs, often of Lebanese descent, who made substantial initial investments, if only to finance the necessary (multipurpose or variable) equipment and who have knowledge of what is going on in neighbouring countries. Instead of relying on protection they have gone for innovation and competition. The

Table 4.3 Average of six industrial subsectors Burkina Faso, 1991

Variables	Sample	1	2	3	4	5	6
Turnover (annually)	1486	1721	5782	508	1156	267	752
Govt participation (%)	19.12	21.91	37.83	33.33	26.58	0.90	3.77
Foreign participation (%)	23.67	19.67	11.83	22.50	32.42	15.10	35.56
Capital	330	328	1378	232	100	61	304
Investments	478	757	1378	240	247	115	498
Total employment	112.3	130.7	362.2	45.8	65.8	27.5	121.9
Exports (% of turnover)	16.12	30.08	30.17	47.67	1.25	0.10	4.78
Valued added (% of total)	26.15	17.08	37.33	35.33	24.00	35.70	16.89
Capacity utilized (%)	46.19	56.92	53.80	13.60	50.67	40.00	43.22
Capital intensity (CFA/emp)	4.82	5.43	1.85	4.07	3.39	4.51	8.77
Productivity (turnover/emp)	9.99	9.30	5.32	16.87	10.83	5.72	13.02
Age enterprise (years)	11.4	12.6	12.0	19.3	13.2	7.5	6.3
Profitability (%)	52.7	41.7	33.3	33.3	58.3	80.0	55.6
Number	55	12	6	6	12	10	9

Note: The figures indicate millions of CFA francs, unless otherwise indicated.

Table 4.4 A comparison of flexible specialization and other firms

Variables	Flexible	Other firms	Significance
Turnover (annually)	514	1926	0.000
Govt participation (%)	6.25	25.05	0.059
Foreign participation (%)	30.75	26.4	(0.138)
Capital	89	435	0.000
Investments	299	624	0.003
Total employment (number)	56.9	140.9	0.000
Exports (% of turnover)	20.25	18.13	(0.476)
Value added (% of total)	22.25	24.23	(0.263)
Capacity utilized (%)	67.12	42.00	(0.797)
Capital intensity (CFA/emp)	5.24	5.54	(0.718)
Productivity (turnover/emp)	8.08	11.59	0.001
Age enterprise (years)	10.1	12.1	(0.178)
Profitability (%)	62.5	42.5	n.s.

Note: The figures indicate million CFA francs, unless otherwise indicated. The significance is the chance of the F-value in the case of a two-tailed t-test for the difference between two means. The chances put between brackets are considered not significant. 100CFA=2 French francs, which is roughly US$0.33.

competition with legal or illegal imports is particularly tough, and due to the economic crisis of the eighties, a number of modern industrial enterprises went bankrupt. Some of the survivors were forced to innovate, and to increase local supplies instead of continuing to import products, and to work with other local firms. These entrepreneurs have stressed innovation, subcontracting and competitiveness with each other and with imported products. Table 4.4 compares the eight firms following the flexible specialization approach with the other 47 units.

The table shows that the industries following the flexible specialization approach are generally smaller in terms of investments, employment and turnover. They are also somewhat younger, have less government participation in their capital and more foreign capital participation. Explanatory variables seem to be the higher level of capacity utilization, a higher percentage of turnover exported, while the percentage of value added in the turnover is somewhat lower, suggesting that subcontracting takes place more often. The capital intensity is somewhat lower (n.s.), while the productivity of labour is significantly lower, suggesting that the firms following the flexible specialization approach use more labour. This reflects the scarcity of capital in Burkina versus the abundance of labour. The percentage of firms following the flexible specialization approach and making profit is higher.

New competition in Burkina Faso's modern industrial sector

The eight new competition enterprises were also found in the subsectors of metal, woodworking and fruits and vegetables, but also some in the

Table 4.5 A comparison of new competition and other firms

Variables	New competition	Others	Significance
Turnover (annually)	849	1859	0.000
Govt participation (%)	10.11	24.30	(0.594)
Foreign participation (%)	13.75	29.80	(0.759)
Capital	135	426	0.001
Investments	316	621	0.003
Total employment (number)	78.5	136.6	0.001
Exports (% of turnover)	34.88	15.20	(0.541)
Value added (% of total)	23.50	23.97	(0.493)
Capacity utilized (%)	62.25	42.98	(0.871)
Capital intensity (CFA/emp)	3.99	5.79	(0.379)
Productivity (turnover/emp)	8.85	11.43	0.005
Age enterprise (years)	10.0	12.1	(0.346)
Profitability (%)	62.50	42.50	n.s.

Note: The figures indicate million CFA francs, unless otherwise indicated. The significance is the chance of the F-value in the case of a two-tailed t-test for the difference between two means.

chemical and textiles subsectors. Table 4.5 compares the new competition companies with the others. It shows that the new competition industries are also generally smaller in terms of investments, employment and turnover. They are also somewhat younger and have less government and foreign participation in their capital. Important explanatory variables seem to be the higher level of capacity utilization and the higher percentage of turnover exported, while the capital intensity and the productivity of labour are significantly lower in the case of new competition firms. The percentage of firms following the new competition approach and making a profit is again higher.

Industrial estates in Burkina Faso

Finally we compare the industries located at the three industrial estates with the others to determine the importance of that kind of clustering for modern industries.

Now the picture changes drastically. Table 4.6 shows that the industries located on the three industrial estates of Burkina are generally bigger in terms of investments, employment and turnover. They have more government participation in their capital and significantly more foreign participation in their capital. An important variable seems to be the lower percentage of turnover exported, which indicates that these are often import-substitution industries. Striking also is the percentage of value added in the turnover, which is lower suggesting simple processing units. The capital intensity is significantly higher, likewise the productivity of labour, which probably reflects the higher investments and the more capital

Table 4.6 Industries located on industrial estates and others

Variables	Estate	Others	Significance
Turnover (annually)	2217	413	0.000
Govt participation (%)	22.71	20.00	(0.867)
Foreign participation (%)	34.32	9.64	0.022
Capital	491	102	0.000
Investments	726	190	0.000
Total employment (number)	156.2	55.7	0.000
Exports (% of turnover)	6.71	47.07	0.000
Value added (% of total)	21.17	30.05	0.008
Capacity utilized (%)	47.18	43.79	(0.795)
Capital intensity (CFA/emp)	6.36	3.37	0.044
Productivity (turnover/emp)	11.15	10.64	(0.548)
Age enterprise (years)	11.4	12.5	(0.650)
Profitability (%)	42.86	47.06	n.s.

Note: The figures indicate millions CFA francs, unless otherwise indicated. The significance is the chance of the F-value in the case of a two-tailed t-test for the difference between two means.

intensive nature of production. The firms are less often profitable, however. Remarkably, only one-quarter of the new competition firms are located in the industrial estates, while this is the case in fifty per cent of the firms following the flexible specialization approach.

Conclusion

Aspects that do not receive sufficient attention in structure–conduct–performance theory are the importance of government policies (at the national and the local level – at present the theory stresses only competition policies), of stimulating interfirm division of labour and the role of co-operation within a competitive framework. The role of interfirm relations is also not sufficiently analysed.[9] Subjects that do receive too much importance in the structure–conduct–performance paradigm are market structures, particularly the role of monopolies and cartels. Japan can be mentioned as a case of co-existence of imperfect competition and cartels and a growing, innovating economy.

There is no lack of disruptive circumstances in Burkina Faso, nor of adaptation by the modern industrialists. Besides *coups d'état* and heavy government interference in the economy, the market has been flooded by industrial products dumped by some Asian NICs. This has led to the disappearance of a certain number of industrial enterprises. Only a small part of the reactions to these changes can be classified as flexible specialization or new competition. Flexible specialization may have a better chance in the future, given the increasing importance of small enterprises in the economy, the effects of the economic crisis of the eighties in the modern

Table 4.7 Recommendations for industrial development in Burkina Faso

- Support the creation of a centre for innovation and quality improvement, helping entrepreneurs with product design, improvement of production methods and the optimal use of multi-purpose equipment.
- Recommend the use of multi-purpose equipment, particularly in the smaller production units and promote their introduction.
- Promote clusters of enterprises of different sizes and working in different industries. For example, reserve space for smaller units in the existing industrial zones, where co-operative competition would be possible.
- Stimulate the formation of networks of entrepreneurs.
- Support subcontracting arrangements as a way to reinforce the industrial tissue.
- Vocational training is important and needs to enhance an innovative mentality. It should explain possibilities of starting small and medium enterprises.

industrial sector and the actual competition of imported goods. Export possibilities, assumed by the new competition, hardly exist for Burkina, however, except for some exports to neighbouring countries. There are also few large-scale entrepreneurial firms willing to experiment with vertical disintegration or different modes of organization. But there is certainly more scope for subcontracting, more interfirm division of labour and promoting networks or clusters.

The analysis has shown that the firms following flexible specialization and the new competition approach are the smaller and the younger ones with less government participation in their capital. They tend to export more and use their equipment more frequently and are consequently more often profitable. More structural characteristics are the lower capital intensity of these firms, the lower productivity in terms of turnover per employee and the lower value added as percentage of turnover. At the industrial estates of Burkina we find the somewhat older and definitely larger firms. These are often the firms in which the government participates and which have been established for import substitution purposes, or to increase the value added of locally produced raw materials. Only half of the firms following the flexible specialization approach can be found on these industrial estates and only a quarter of the new competition firms.

What is the relevance of these new ideas for developing countries like Indonesia and Burkina Faso? The importance of the new competition is that it stresses the dynamic role of the entrepreneurial firm in the economy and the necessity to create the conditions for this kind of firm to play that role. It also forces one to think about a number of interrelated issues, which are normally not discussed in relation to each other: the globalization of the economy, competition and collaboration and the role of small, medium and large enterprises. The strength of flexible specialization is its attention to technology, innovation and craftsmanship.

The question remains – which combination of economic, social and institutional arrangements can provide the conditions enabling small, medium and large-scale firms in developing countries to compete successfully on national and international markets? Flexible specialization and the new competition can become an industrialization strategy to recommend even in Burkina Faso (Van Dijk, 1991; and 1992b). The notion of industrial districts will still have to be developed. The present industrial estates certainly do not serve that purpose. Table 4.7 gives a summary of the recommendations made to achieve this kind of industrial development in Burkina Faso (Van Dijk, 1991).

The concepts of flexible specialization and new competition provide possibilities for bridging the gap between general economics with a focus on macroeconomic growth and the importance of world market developments and business economics with a interest in firm and industry level variables.

ASIAN EXPERIENCES

5 Lack of interaction between traders and producers in the Agra footwear cluster

PETER KNORRINGA

Introduction[1]

This paper deals with flexible specialization in an Indian cluster, industrial networks within that cluster, and the actors within those industrial networks. Flexible specialization is seen as a particular strategy for competitive success based on efficient and flexible production and marketing of quality-competitive products (Asheim, 1992). Such a concept becomes operational only when linked to specific actors. Agra, a city in India of 1.5 million inhabitants, is characterized by a geographical concentration of footwear manufacturers and their relevant linkage units, and is an example *par excellence* of a cluster. Within this cluster one can distinguish five types of networks in which small-scale production units participate. Such networks are led by actors, whether traders or trader-producers, who set the boundary conditions for production and marketing of the final product. To some extent, these leading actors can choose to pursue a flexible specialization strategy, in contrast to a strategy based on low-quality, low-cost products, combined with sweated labour.

Agra is a good example of flexible specialization in developing countries in terms of intensive subcontracting and selective collaboration within networks and among enterprises, as well as widespread skills among workers. However, it is a less good example of flexible specialization in terms of innovation and constant quality improvement. On the whole, one does not find many leading actors pursuing a flexible specialization strategy. Such a strategy requires a continuous interaction between marketing and production. Skills in marketing and production are seldom combined in one person. Therefore, co-operation based on trust between actors with those distinct skills is seen as the key towards a flexible specialization strategy, both within and between firms. In this paper it is argued that a lack of interaction between marketing and production, or, in other words, a lack of perceived interdependency among those actors involved in either marketing or production, is the missing link in Agra's footwear industry.

The flexible specialization debate has shifted attention from individual (small) firms to whole clusters of firms. However, not all firms within a cluster actually have linkages with all other firms. In this paper the focus is on specific industrial networks in which firms interact directly, rather than on the cluster as a whole. The network level of analysis is also preferred to the level of the individual enterprise, but for another reason. Irregularity is the main characteristic of footwear production in Agra. Irregularities in orders received and consequently in employment generated, from season to season, but also from week to week. Due to this irregularity, production units can be open one week and closed the next. Another important irregularity is that persons involved in footwear production can be entrepreneurs of their family-based unit one week, unemployed the next week and working as hired labourers the following week. Therefore, enterprises are the most unstable factor in the industrial structure of Agra.

Therefore, if one's main interest lies in studying the structure of the cluster and its implications on the various categories of participants, one should focus primarily on the network level of analysis, because it is at this level that the strategic decisions are taken by the leading actors. The next step is to see how the formulation of such strategies by the leading actors is influenced by the socio-cultural setting.

The paper is structured along these lines. In the second section the cluster as a whole is introduced. The next section focuses on the specific networks within the cluster, to explain the crucial lack of interaction between marketing and production. Interaction is shown to vary by type of network, and interaction based on trust is found to increase the opportunities for a flexible specialization strategy. However, the fourth section shows that interaction based on trust is rare because the main groups involved in the industry are from very distinct socio-cultural backgrounds. Finally, some conclusions from the previous sections are integrated.

The Agra cluster

Footwear is the main source of livelihood in Agra. Compared to other main footwear centres in India, Agra offers the largest variation in types of production units and traders.[2] The spatial concentration of footwear activities is so high, and the relative importance of this branch to the Agra economy so great, that Agra can be characterized as the most important footwear cluster in India.

The many varieties of footwear are produced in all sorts of enterprises: modern small-scale factories with conveyer belts, traditional workshops with one or two hand-operated machines, or in homes with women workers, and mostly by a combination of the various types of producers. The Agra cluster is not merely a multiplication of producers making similar products. It holds all kinds of specializations, and an inter-firm division of labour has started to develop. Middlemen arrange for the smooth functioning of the system, paid on commission either by larger producers or traders. The approximately 5000 production units are linked to each other through various types of subcontracting arrangements. Apart from enterprises producing more or less finished products there is a large number of very small workshops, with usually only two or three male workers, which undertake specific operations, such as printing and stamping of brand names, or buffing or polishing.

The employment generated by the footwear industry in Agra is much larger than the 60,000 people directly involved in production (see Table 5.1). In the larger units there are the owners, managers, administrative staff and supervisors. There is a flourishing industry of suppliers to the footwear industry, employing a few thousand people, such as makers of leatherboard, of counters and stiffeners, of lasts, and of cardboard boxes. Another 1000 to 1500 persons find employment in trade. These are the suppliers of raw materials to the footwear industry; the raw material dealers, housed in small roadside stalls up to those in fancy offices with air-conditioning. The same continuum applies to the marketing of footwear: the private traders and their helpers, the quality checkers, and so on. Most of the traders are

Table 5.1 Overview of footwear sector in Agra

	Percentage share of categories of production units in:				
	Number of enterprises	Labour force	% of women	Daily production	Daily turnover
Large scale and modern SSI	5	20	20%	40	55
Larger workshops	10	20	–	25	30
Small workshops	25	20	–	15	10
Home-based units	60	25	*)	20	5
Women homeworkers		15	100%		
Estimated absolute totals	5000 units	60,000 persons	13,500 persons	300,000 pairs	Rs. 36 million

Notes: The following working classification is used:

– Large-scale and modern SSI (small-scale industry): Large-scale enterprises in Agra are composed of 8 to 10 production units each, officially independent small-scale units, sometimes within one building. As they fall under central ownership they are referred to in this paper as the large enterprises. Modern SSI are registered small-scale units, with 50 to 100 workers each, which often have some modern machines and electricity.

– Larger workshops are units with only wage labour, employing more than 10 workers and using a mix of modern and traditional technology.

– Small workshops are units with primarily wage labour, employing fewer than 10 persons and using mainly traditional technology.

– Home-based units, with a workplace in or around the home, use primarily or only family labour and mainly traditional technology. This group includes the cottage industries.

– Women homeworkers undertake labour-intensive hand operations on piece rates in their homes.

*) = In home-based units there are only part-time women workers, who assist in specific operations.

Source: Knorringa 1991.

concentrated in one market area in Central Agra, Hing ki Mandi. Apart from this daily market there is a much cheaper place to buy materials and sell intermediary products, Chakipat market, which is held two mornings a week. There are also a few hundred government employees involved in the marketing, checking and promotion of footwear, as well as in running three training institutes. A last category of employment generated by the footwear industry includes the transport and insurance of goods.

Agra traditionally specialized in producing Oxford and Derby shoes (classically styled dress shoes with laces), but in the last five to ten years ladies' Ballerinas, Moccasins and Loafers have become popular. More than 50 per cent of the small enterprises are now producing these new types of footwear or a mix of new and older types (Knorringa, 1991). In the export market Agra is oriented towards the cheap market segments in Western Europe and the USA, but especially towards the medium market segments of the Gulf countries and the ex-Eastern bloc.[3] The main export item produced at the moment are ladies' Ballerinas, which were fashionable and expensive in Europe and the USA five to ten years ago, and at that time mainly produced in Italy and Spain. At present, cheap imitations, produced with third-grade leathers, are mass-produced in Agra for amazingly cheap prices. These previously fashionable shoes are now found in shops in Europe for around $20. They are mainly exported indirectly, through trading houses or large industrial producers from India. Such houses have their purchasing offices in Agra. They pay around $4 to 5 a pair to the principal producer, and sell to retail chains in Europe for around $10. According to international standards Agra is specialized in producing low-cost, low-quality imitations of internationally successful designs which are marketed at the low fashion end of the market.

On the domestic market the most important shift in demand concerns the growth of the more expensive domestic market segment, bolstered by the emerging middle class in India. This domestic market segment is equal or superior to the cheap export market segment, in terms of average quality and price. The type of footwear produced for this market segment is mainly the same, i.e. Loafers and Moccasins. Quantitatively the traditional Oxford and Derby shoes remain most important.

Overall, Agra is known for its hand-made, labour-intensive, medium and low-priced, leather-upper full shoes. Its competitiveness depends completely on its very cheap, abundantly available and highly-skilled labour force, working predominantly with traditional technology.

Networks within Agra

Within Agra distinct networks of firms can be discerned, often oriented to particular market segments. In this section it will be shown that interaction between actors varies according to the network in which it takes place. In general, leading actors of networks that aim at higher market segments offer more favourable forward conditions to their suppliers (Knorringa, 1991). In turn, such favourable conditions instigate more interaction and that creates more options for a flexible specialization strategy.

An industrial network is defined as a group of production units and traders with their relevant linkage units, who constitute a complete marketing and production cycle for a particular set of products (Knorringa and Weijland, 1992). Within a subsector (Boomgard *et al.*, 1992) or a branch (Schmitz, 1982) one usually finds a limited number of types of networks, oriented to specific market segments. Such industrial networks are characterized by repeated transactions between and among production units and traders who, in a constant power play, jointly perform the range of activities needed to complete an entire marketing and production cycle. The cycle consists of the following activities that can be analytically distinguished. To start with, relevant information on existing or potential demand has to be collected. Only after identifying the market situation can product specifications be determined. These preliminary phases condition the organization of production and choice of techniques. Organization and execution of physical production come next, followed by trading and transport of products. This involves detailed price setting, promotion and distribution.

Control of a complete marketing and production cycle does not require ownership and/or management of all activities. A leading entrepreneur, whether a 'pure' trader or a trader-producer, can control an entire cycle by setting the boundary conditions for production and marketing of the final product. Through superior access to information and resources, leading entrepreneurs can determine product specifications and set price ranges in accordance with the selected market segments. Leading entrepreneurs decide whether and when to use distinct categories of small enterprises. They can select 'suitable' small enterprises, and incorporate them into 'their' industrial networks. They exert control over small enterprises by fixing standards for inputs and outputs, they might provide materials and equipment, and sometimes offer advance payments for production. In such cases leading firms can make small enterprises entirely dependent. Thus, leading firms can reap the gains of low-cost production by small enterprises, while keeping control over the entire production process. Market agents are the direct link between small enterprises and the leading firms in the more complex industrial networks. In the context of this study, market agents are seen as 'representing' distinct networks. Market agents bargain with the various types of small enterprises on forward conditions related to specific orders. The actual forward conditions are a reflection of the bargaining position of distinct small enterprises. The case study presented in this paper focuses only on specific linkages between these market agents and small-scale final producers. That is not to say that other linkages, e.g. among small producers, or between small producers and (government) institutions, are not important (see Knorringa, 1991).

The interaction between market agents and small enterprises can be analysed within the framework of the 'new institutional economics', of which the transaction-cost approach (Williamson, 1975; 1985) is one of the main strands. Williamson has set a research agenda by presenting the market versus hierarchy dichotomy. The leading question in his framework is how to keep opportunistic behaviour of transaction partners in check; in case of 'pure' markets this is achieved through prices, while 'pure' hierarchies are governed solely by authority. From this starting point many authors have assumed a continuum between markets and hierarchies (for developing countries, see Mead, 1984). Nevertheless, the mainstream transaction-costs approach claims that, in the final analysis, all forms of economic organization can be reduced to either market or hierarchy.

However, several recent contributions to economic literature conclude that within the dichotomy it is not possible to deal satisfactorily with co-operation among firms in networks in which repeated transactions, in some cases leading to trust relations, take place.[4] It has been argued that such long-term voluntary patterns of co-operation, both among and within firms, do not fit well in the dichotomy, nor can they be placed on the continuum (Knorringa and Kox, 1992). Such co-operation is first of all characterized by the recognition of interdependency by both transaction partners. This recognition, and the behaviour it instigates, leads to an essentially distinct way of restraining opportunism, namely a degree of trust based on a thorough knowledge of each others situation. To be clear, this is not the type of trust based on idealism or naiveté, but a trust based on the realization by specialists that they need each other, in such a way that they will also have to trust each other to some extent. In the transaction-cost approach the critical issue is not that all actors are assumed to behave opportunistically, but that it is very costly to find out who will and who will not behave opportunistically (Williamson and Ouchi, 1981). It is the presence of mutual familiarity and trust that enables a transaction partner to consciously take uninsured risks.[5] Thus, trust lowers the transaction costs as it increases the predictability of the others' behaviour.

Several indications suggest that relations supplemented with trust, *ceteris paribus*, lead to better performance in the longer run and lower the threat of opportunistic behaviour. The success of Japanese and more recently Italian industrialization strategies has shown the importance of voluntary co-operation (see Best, 1990; Pyke, Becattini and Sengenberger, 1990). Best claims that the basic reason for Japanese companies and 'The Third Italy' to outperform the large bureaucratic companies, based on Taylorist management and Fordist production methods, is that they have succeeded in finding a better balance between competition and co-operation. To get more grip on this balance we need to include the concepts of voluntary co-operation and trust in our analysis.[6]

In short, in transaction patterns based on voluntary co-operation, opportunistic behaviour is restrained in a way which is essentially different from 'pure' market or hierarchical co-ordination. Therefore, one might perceive of three principles of co-ordination: market, hierarchy and co-operation, controlled respectively through prices, authority and trust (see also Bradach and Eccles, 1989; Powell, 1989). The resulting triangle is shown in Figure 5.1. This triangle essentially means that any relation between specific actors is not characterised by either hierarchy, market or co-operation, but by a mix of these three. The hypothesis is that the mix of market, hierarchy and co-operation is influenced by the market segment to which the network is geared, in such a way that production for a higher market segment results in a mix that is more dominated by co-operation.

In the footwear industry in Agra there are five types of networks in which small enterprises participate (Knorringa, 1991). Each letter in Figure 5.1 depicts an exchange relation between a small-scale final producer and its direct market agent. The placement of the specific linkages within the triangle is tentative and qualitative.

Linkage **a** is between the smallest household units and local wholesalers. These household units, based on family labour and primitive technology, produce basic cheap shoes with traditional designs. The head of the

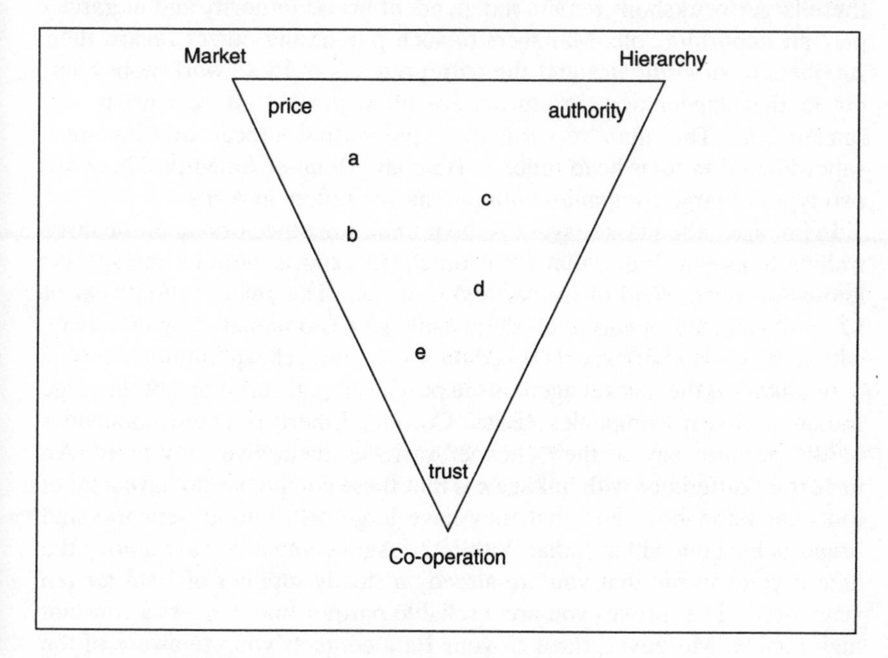

Figure 5.1 *Principles of co-ordination*

household goes to the market two or three times a week where he tries to sell to local wholesalers. Most wholesalers need some of those basic shoes now and then, but there are always a lot of suppliers in this segment. The household units must sell, to be able to buy new inputs. Therefore, margins are pushed to the minimum, producers remain anonymous and their products are rather homogeneous. Bargaining is actually only on the price, as production has already been carried out.

Linkage **b** is between somewhat more specialized household units and small workshops (five to ten wage labourers), on the one hand, and local wholesalers, on the other hand. Entrepreneurs in this segment try to get orders from those local wholesalers. In this segment there is no longer anonymity of producers, nor homogeneity of products. Product specifications are discussed in advance, samples are made, quality of the product is higher, quantities are larger, and payments are no longer in cash. In short, both actors invest in their mutual linkage. A certain degree of trust develops over time, but as there is still a large number of technically competitive suppliers, the price mechanism remains dominant in most cases.

Linkages of the types **a** and **b** exist already for decades in Agra (Lynch, 1969; Leest, 1984). More recently developed linkages are those of type **c** and **d**. These deal with linkages between larger workshops (10 to 50 labourers) and purchasing offices of large companies. Although officially these larger workshops remain independent firms, authority and hierarchy play an important role. Managers of such purchasing offices regard their suppliers as subordinates and the entrepreneurs of these workshops comply to that expectation. Producers are often pushed into exclusivity arrangements. The managers of such purchasing offices are, in turn, subordinated to their head office in Bombay, Delhi or Calcutta. There are two types of large companies with purchasing offices in Agra.

In linkage **c** the market agent is the purchasing office of one of the large trading houses in India, that focus on cheap exports without any specific know-how in the field of leather and footwear. This refers to footwear of $15 to 20 in a European retail shop. Linkage **c** is dominated by hierarchy, within the context of exports based on low-quality, cheap imitations.

In linkage **d** the market agent is the purchasing officer of one of the large Indian footwear companies (Bata, Corona, Liberty). These companies hardly produce any of their cheaper varieties themselves any more. An important difference with linkage **c** is that these companies do have a lot of footwear know-how, and that they have large distribution networks and brand-name goodwill in India. Within the Agra context you are among the elite if you can say that you are already a steady supplier of Bata for ten years or so. That proves you are a reliable partner that delivers a constant high quality. Moreover, through your Bata contacts you are aware of the latest technological and marketing developments. In the case of **d**, much more than with **c**, the hierarchy gives way to a linkage in which trust has become more important.

The last linkage shown in Figure 5.1 is that of type **e**. This linkage deals with the modern small direct exporters (25 to 10 wage labourers). Entrepreneurs of such enterprises themselves go to international leather fairs with their latest designs and try to establish contacts with buyers for retail chains. The shoes are priced between $75 and 100 in the shop. Entrepreneurs maintain direct telephone and fax contact with Frankfurt and Paris. In the eyes of the European and American buyers the most crucial characteristic of an Indian supplier in this market segment is his reliability; that he supplies what he promised. And not, as often happens in linkage **c**, using inferior materials or shaky stitching work on the second or third delivery. In short, linkage **e** evolves around trust. Of course, price plays a role and the linkage is not free from authority feelings, but the dominant factor is the realization of the need for mutual trust.

At this point it is important to note that by far most producers face linkages without a significant degree of trust. Only some 25 small-scale units (0.5 per cent of all small production units) transact with market agents in the way depicted by linkage type **e**. Approximately 2 per cent of all small production units work for one of the large Indian footwear companies (linkage type **d**). The large majority of the small producers in the Agra cluster face linkages dominated by the market mechanism: linkage type **a** (35 per cent), or **b** (55 per cent).

The aim of this section has been to show how interaction varies between networks. In the case of Agra we find that some networks are co-ordinated in a more hierarchical manner, while others are more based on market co-ordination or co-operation. Even within one network there can be distinct mixes in the principles of co-ordination. The network leader might have a linkage based primarily on trust with one of his essential suppliers, while the relation with low-skilled, readily-available household units is much more co-ordinated through authority. Therefore, it would be an over-simplification to describe whole clusters as either hierarchical or co-operative in types of linkages.

Voluntary co-operation between actors appears to be a necessary, though not sufficient condition for a flexible specialization strategy. Such co-operation, enabling the development of trust, is usually found only in the higher market segments. In Agra, however, only a very small number of leading actors aim for these higher market segments. Most leading actors aim at lower market segments, focusing not on quality improvement and product development, but primarily on price reductions and short-term profits. So, most leading actors do not pursue a flexible specialization strategy. Therefore, the small production units in these networks are faced with linkages dominated either by price or authority considerations, and cannot benefit from trust.

The lack of interaction is by no means influenced only by the type of network in which it takes place. The main groups involved in the industry, traditionally-skilled artisans and commercially-trained entrepreneurs, do not communicate unless they must, because they belong to very distinct socio-economic strata. That is the subject of the next section.

Makers and sellers of footwear

In this section we turn to the participating groups of actors and their perceived conflicting interests. In India, the people involved in trade and production of footwear are from a different caste background. Trade in footwear is dominated by Hindus from forward castes with Punjabi or Sindhi background, and Muslims. The actual making of footwear is a sub-caste specific occupation in the sense that only those born as Chamars 'can occupy the status of shoe maker without breaking caste rules' (Lynch, 1969:15). In the traditional caste system, Chamars are close to the bottom of the hierarchy because they work with a polluting object, leather, and because they are reputed to eat beef, the most polluting of foods according to orthodox Hinduism (Khare, 1984; Sharma, 1986). Although nation-wide most Chamars are agricultural labourers and do not work with leather, most leather workers are Chamars. In Agra footwear workers are predominantly Jatavs, a subgroup of the Chamars. For the Jatavs footwear is a way of life. There is no easy alternative to their traditional occupation, so that their social and economic options are severely limited. Apart from Jatavs some poorer sections of the Muslim community are also involved in footwear making. However, Muslims in the footwear industry are relatively much more involved in trade and as entrepreneurs running workshops in which sometimes Muslims but predominantly Jatavs work.

Up to the 1960s, production used to take place almost exclusively in household enterprises, of which the Jatav head of the household would sell the produced pairs to a local trader who would sell to outside merchants. These traders, and other newcomers to the footwear industry, have now also started to set up production units. In this way they have gradually displaced the 'big men' in the Jatav community. According to Lynch (1969:39): 'These new higher caste entrepreneurs can, if necessary, freeze out a lower-caste competitor by making salient the Jatavs' untouchable status within the market networks'. Most of these new entrepreneurs can be seen as financier entrepreneurs, as opposed to the more traditional Jatav master artisans, whose master status is based on technical skills. The main reason for this shift was the need felt by traders to be able to more directly control production. The type of production units that they run are larger workshops and small modern factories. In such units the entrepreneurs deal directly with a number of Jatav group leaders on piece rate orders. These group leaders are mostly ex-entrepreneurs of household enterprises. They again distribute the work among their old workers, usually from the same *mohalla* and often kin related. This means that caste differences, and the subsequent tensions, that used to exist mainly between the trader and the producer, have to some extent shifted to the relations within the larger workshops and small factories.

At the same time, this has a bearing on the development of trust relations between traders and entrepreneurs of production units. Linkage type **a**, between household units and local traders, represents the classical case of the (Jatav) master artisan dealing with the forward caste trader. Entrepreneurs of production units that face linkage type **b** are from various backgrounds. They are, firstly, the more successful artisans, often more 'separated' from involvement in direct production, who run small and some larger workshops, and, secondly, the trader-entrepreneurs, originating from footwear trading communities. Entrepreneurs of production units that market their products to the purchasing offices of export trading housed (linkage type **c**), are predominantly young, educated middle class males, without any significant experience in footwear trade or production. Most of them have a degree in commerce and they have entered the industry with the expectation of the heaps of gold to be earned from exporting cheap leather-upper footwear. This background is similar to most of the staff members at the trading-house purchasing offices. Next are the entrepreneurs of production units that market their produce to the purchasing offices of the large Indian footwear companies (linkage type **d**). They have either a commercial or an engineering background and are well-established and experienced in the industry, as are their counterparts, the staff members of the Bata, Corona or Liberty purchasing offices. Linkage type **e**, the only linkage where the entrepreneur of the small production unit deals directly with foreign buyers, requires trust to get started in the first place. Thus, the people involved in this linkage already knew and trusted each other, and that enabled the linkage to emerge.

On the cluster level of analysis, however, the basic fact remains that the Jatavs know how to make shoes, and that the forward caste traders or entrepreneurs know how to market shoes. At the same time, the traders and trader-entrepreneurs have no eye for changes in the production process, while the artisans have no eye for changes in product specifications. Both groups are highly adaptable within their own environment, but the two worlds do not meet to combine their knowledge. Jatavs are treated roughly and with disdain by traders and contacts are kept to an absolute minimum. There are no linkages between Jatavs and forward caste traders in which **trust** plays a role.

The traders respond to demand from outside by taking orders for the lowest price and leaving the production to the Jatavs. The traders squeeze the Jatavs as much as they can through low piece rates. The traders try to maintain their margins, in a situation of decreasing prices for final products, through squeezing labour and material costs. The Jatavs respond by producing the lowest quality that is acceptable to traders, either because these traders are unaware of the fact that inferior and cheaper materials are used, or they are indifferent to it. So, both groups are not so much taking initiative as responding to pressures. The difference is that for the traders it is an offensive strategy, while for the Jatavs it is a defensive strategy. In effect there is a power struggle, mostly below the surface, between the two groups instead of a realization of the need to co-operate. In case marketing and production skills would be combined, the bargaining position of Agra towards the 'outside' world would be improved substantially. This power struggle between the 'makers' and the 'sellers' is also a basic difference with the Third Italy case studies, where there is supposed to be no such internal chasm between the 'carriers' of these two types of knowledge, as the artisans and the traders are the same, or at least from the same community.[7] However, in Agra they fight each other instead of the competition, for example, from Indonesia or China.

One cynical result of this internal struggle is that new initiatives by the most innovative leading actors of networks are based on a strategy towards Taylorism, not flexible specialization. The few entrepreneurs that have started to aim for higher quality market segments, disregard the traditionally skilled labourers and, instead, set up larger factories with modern machines, conveyer belts, and unskilled but obedient women workers. These entrepreneurs, from forward caste background or Muslims, feel that Jatav artisans are more of a burden than an asset to the development of the footwear industry in Agra. This means that the strongest point of Agra, the abundant availability of cheap **skilled** labour from an artisanal background, is not considered an asset by leading actors who shape the strategy for the future. Pursuing the Taylorist/Fordist option means that Agra would become just another cheap labour cluster with mainly semi-skilled factory workers.

Conclusion

Agra is the most important footwear cluster in India. The cluster as a whole specializes in labour-intensive, cheap shoes, imitations of internationally successful designs. Most leading actors – in Agra those from forward caste with a commercial background – do not focus on quality improvement and product development, but primarily on price reductions and short-term profits. In combination with the surplus labour situation, this has led to a spiral of lower prices, lower costs and lower wages in a substantial part of the cluster. So, there are ample indications that most leading actors in Agra do not pursue a flexible specialization strategy.

The key towards a flexible specialization strategy is interaction between marketing and production. In Agra, the main reason for the lack of interaction is a power struggle between traditionally skilled artisans ('makers') and commercially trained entrepreneurs ('sellers'). This power struggle is due to a perception of conflicting interests, instead of interdependencies. It is up to the strongest party in this struggle, the leading actors, to take the first step in recognizing mutual interdependencies, so that interaction between marketing and production can develop.

6 The impact of technological change on interfirm linkages

A case study of clustered rural small-scale roof tile enterprises in Central Java

HENRY SANDEE

A significant part of rural industrial enterprise in the province of Central Java, Indonesia, is clustered. Differences between clusters may be substantial, even when they belong to the same industrial subsector. In some clusters, the technology used may be fairly simple, production units traditional, and products cheap, aimed at poor consumers in the direct neighbourhood. In other clusters of the same industrial subsector, output may be of a much more sophisticated nature, and directed towards urban, or even export, markets for consumers with high incomes.

Enterprises within a certain cluster have a large number of economic, social and cultural characteristics. The same technology is used, prices and quality of output do not differ very much, and production is often aimed at the same segment of the market. A cluster is generally located in a village which has its own specific social and cultural background. However, this homogeneity should not close our eyes to the existence of inequality among firms of the cluster. These differences may not only reflect their efficiency but may also be a consequence of their differing degrees of vertical integration (Liedholm and Mead, 1987; Smyth, 1990; White, 1992). Many producers are in fact not entrepreneurs in the proper sense of the term. Economic, and also social and cultural differences may be revealed by attending to networks and inequality structure, and the way in which distinct enterprises are embedded in them.

Introduction of new technology in a cluster will influence the organization of production and marketing. Adoption and diffusion of more productive equipment may disturb existing networks and inequality structure, and have consequences for the linkages among enterprises themselves. This paper discusses the nature of interfirm linkages in different technological settings. The impact of technological change is studied for a tile cluster in the village of Karanggeneng, in the Boyolali regency of Central Java. An important question is whether innovation can be integrated into existing networks and interfirm linkages, or whether it leads to changes in the organization of production and marketing.

This paper focuses on the manufacturing of roofing tiles in rural Central Java. The next section presents a brief overview of the tile subsector, as well as the overall research project to which this case study belongs. The tile cluster of Karanggeneng is introduced, and interfirm linkages in the years before adoption and diffusion of more productive technology are discussed. The impact of new technology on traditional interfirm linkages is then analysed partly based on earlier papers by Knorringa and Sandee (1990) and Sandee (1990). Finally, the outcomes of the Karanggeneng case study are briefly compared with developments in two other clusters which have preceded it in its change from traditional to more productive, so called intermediate, technology.

Rural tiles production and marketing in Central Java: A subsector approach

The overall research project, to which this case study belongs, uses a subsector approach within specific regional settings, concentrating on the impact of innovation on interfirm linkages and networks in clusters with different locations and market outlets. The subsector concept facilitates analysis of technological development in relation to market development, as it refers to firms which in theory would be able to produce identical products, but with economic development tend to show increasing differentiation, both in product quality and in technology. Increasing market segmentation within the subsector is associated with increasing technological hierarchy (Boomgard *et al.*, 1992).

A classification of technology that coincides with the hierarchy given by the structure of demand is used. In rural tile production in Central Java, four discrete technologies are distinguished, ranging from primitive, traditional, and intermediate, to modern mechanized production equipment. Firms belonging to the same technology class tend to cluster in certain locations. The top technical rural level serves the highest market segment and leads qualitative demand development. However, it faces fierce competition from large-scale urban production of tiles. Table 6.1 summarizes characteristics of studied clusters, technologies, and marketing.

In clusters, economic inequality among firms operating with the same technology is determined within networks which give access to markets, finance, as well as set their socio-economic role in the local economy (Rasmussen, 1992). Network leaders have better access to markets, finance, land, and so on, operate in a better entrepreneurial milieu, and have more power. Interfirm linkages are embedded into local networks. The latter encompass interfirm linkages as well as relation between producers and traders, middlemen, suppliers, and institutions.

The overall research project sheds light on the issue to what extent distinct firms, at various levels of technology and in various clusters, profit from clustering through flexible specialization (flexible division of tasks, orders, and/or labour) and collective efficiency (attainment of higher efficiency levels due to nearby physical presence of other producers). Flexible specialization and collective efficiency turn out to be limited among firms

Table 6.1 Characteristics of the rural tiles subsector in Central Java

	Ketoyan	Karang-geneng	Mayong	Klepu	Sokka
1. Regency	Boyolali	Boyolali	Jepara	Klaten	Kebumen
2. Location	Isolated	Near trunk road	Strategic	Strategic	Strategic
3. Technology	Primitive, highly divisible	Traditional, divisible	Intermediate, indivisible	Intermediate, indivisible	Modern, mechanized
4. Labour	Family	Family and wage workers	Family and wage workers	Family and wage workers	Wage workers
5. Scale of enterprise	Household	Small	Small	Medium	Large
6. Networks	Fragmented	Developing	Complex	Complex	Disintegrated
7. Marketing	Small middlemen	Various channels	Various channels	Various channels	Agents
8. Market	Poor rural consumers	Rural and poor urban consumers	Middle income urban consumers	Middle income urban consumers	Middle and high-income urban consumers

within clusters at the lower technology levels. Here micro-firms are an integral part of the multiplicity of jobs undertaken by rural households. Clusters of firms at higher technology levels are more complex. There are more backward and forward linkages and interfirm linkages, allowing firms to arrive at a division of tasks and labour within the cluster. Here, the proximity of others makes it possible to carry out a greater variety of tasks and orders because firms can rely on others during certain stages of the production and marketing cycle. Specialization among firms may be flexible in the sense that different orders lead to different divisions of work among local firms.

Technological change in clusters is a special case, since adoption of new technology does not have to be a decision or action at the individual firm level. In clusters, firms may make use of existing (latent) interfirm linkages and networks, or create new ones to facilitate innovation. The characteristics of both the new technology as well as the economic networks in the cluster determine the pattern of diffusion of innovations among local firms. Pioneer adoption is often characterized by interdependent decisionmaking of a number of firms. The way pioneer adoption comes about is crucial for further diffusion of new technology among firms of clusters. A study of the impact of technological change may show the importance of collective action for technological upgrading. The benefits of such change may not be evenly spread (Smyth, 1990). Change puts local networks under pressure, and diffusion of new technology may result in new processes of differentiation. In principle, several patterns of differentiation can be distinguished:

- Innovations result in a continuation of traditional interfirm linkages and networks. Local leaders remain in control of their network, and the innovation may even allow them to strengthen their position.
- Growing inequality and an increased hierarchy of firms within networks. Leaders increasingly control access to resources and markets. Outcontracting and putting out gain importance, and result in new, hierarchical linkages among producers. Economic differentiation among firms increases overtime, making the distribution of benefits from innovation more and more skewed.
- Concentration of enterprise leads to production on a larger scale. The number of firms within a cluster declines, and a number of small-scale entrepreneurs end up as wage workers for big firms. Networks and interfirm linkages collapse as leading firms are concentrating production and forward and backward linkages under their own roof or management.
- Flexible specialization implying well developed interfirm linkages, with firms looking for partners among adopters whenever orders urge them to do so.

This case study on innovations in the roof tile industry of Karanggeneng tries to analyse the impact of technological change within the framework discussed above, especially on how to interpret processes of differentiation and changes in interfirm linkages.

Decades without change in technology: Karanggeneng before 1988

Karanggeneng is located just outside Boyolali town, which, with 56,000 inhabitants in 1990, is the only urban centre in the Boyolali recency. Prior to 1988, there were some 100 small enterprises in Karanggeneng producing traditional tiles for rural and poor urban consumers. The main characteristics of the production and marketing of traditional tiles are mentioned in Tables 6.1 and 6.2.

Traditional tiles in Karanggeneng are produced in batches. The average capacity of kilns in which tiles are fired is 5000 units, in line with the loading capacity of trucks which transport tiles, directly or indirectly, to consumers. Inputs, most importantly clay and firewood, are bought locally from specialized suppliers. Enterprises buy 'ready inputs' implying that clay has been prepared and wood cut into pieces. Printing and firing tiles is done at the production site, mainly by family labour, with occasional assistance from casual (male) wage labourers. Before firing takes place, tiles are spread out on the ground to dry in the sun. Access to space is of importance. Firms do not market their own output, but tiles are collected at the production site by traders, middlemen, as well as final consumers. All provide producers with advance payments in cash, and middlemen also deliver inputs in kind.

Within enterprises a change of moulds used for printing does occur, dependent on the exact type of traditional tiles that are demanded. The use of another mould does, however, not lead to a change of the intrafirm division of tasks and labour.

Economic inequality among firms in Karanggeneng was noticeable. Enterprises located along the main road through the village were doing better business, produced more output, and reached higher incomes than those located at the outskirts of the village. These differences were not reflected by prices for inputs, prices for outputs, skills of producers, or the size and quality of kiln used. There are some ten clay pits in the village which are owned by farmers. The farmers employ about eight workers per pit. Tile producers order clay in cubic metres and get it delivered at their production site ready for printing. Prices were fixed and no discounts provided for big quantities. Orders are placed with pit owners, and prepared clay is delivered in accordance with the sequence of orders. Prices of output did hardly differ among firms, and also not between distinct market channels. Output prices were standardized, and there was rarely a discussion on prices between producers and buyers. Any occurring price differences were explained by the amount of advance payments received. The larger the advance payments for orders, the lower the prices that buyers would be paying. There was no correlation between total output during the (studied) dry season of 1987 and output unit price, implying that a larger scale of production was not an asset to outcompete others through price competition. Skills of producers were rather similar. They were all well experi-

Table 6.2 Labour use, costs, and value added of traditional tile production in Karanggeneng, 1987 (Rupiah)

5000 tiles (5% breaks during firing) sales 4750 × Rp26		123 500
Length of production cycle		15 days
Costs of inputs		77 000
– Clay	6 000	
– Casual labour	30 000	
– Transport clay	8 000	
– Sand and water	30 000	
– Firewood	30 000	
Casual labour for firing		5 000
Maintenance and repair		1 500
Value added		40 000
Value added per 1000 tiles sold		8 420
Family labour use		150 hrs
Value added per family labour hour		266

Source: Computed from own field surveys, 1987 (dry season).

enced, and have been apprentices at the production sites of their parents, or relatives. Use was made of casual workers during the difficult process of firing tiles. They are specialized and serve all producers in the village. Kilns were very similar, and most were built by the same group of construction workers.

Explanation of economic differences in Karanggeneng starts from the fact that there was much variation in the total number of production runs done through a season or year, although the size of separate runs did not differ much as was mentioned above. A large number of runs allowed certain economies of scale like lower set-up costs, and a more efficient use of casual labour. During the dry season of 1987, leading firms were able to market 24 batches of 5000 tiles, while marginal firms did not sell more than seven batches. A production run in Karanggeneng, on average, is carried out in ten days. This implies that leading firms were actually relying on other producers in the cluster to serve their customers. This points to a crucial characteristic of inequality among firms, that is of unequal access to markets. Leading firms, due to their favourable cash position, were able to offer better terms to customers than other: they were willing to accept smaller amounts of advance payments. Leading firms were able to expand their capacity in case orders exceeded the possibilities at their own production site. Leading firms in the cluster were surrounded by their 'subordinates' which made outcontracting easy given the bulky nature of the production process. Generally, it concerns commercial subcontracting in which orders are fully handed over to and carried out by 'subordinate' firms.

Outcontracting implied that neighbouring firms were used for their labour, space for drying tiles, as well as their kiln capacity. Family ties turn out to be important since leading producers are often surrounded by their relatives which are also active as tiles producers. This gives an additional dimension to interfirm linkages through outcontracting. It often concerns co-operation between members of an extended family. On other occasions, these 'related' firms competed with each other, although prices were hardly ever used as an instrument to outcompete others. Leading firms receive orders and are paid by customers. Subcontracted firms get less for the job than in case they would directly deal with customers. For them, the main advantage of their location close to leading firms is the assurance of regular additional orders on top of their own contracts. Interfirm linkages are centred around outcontracting batches in case own capacity is not sufficient to fulfil demand.

Diffusion of more productive technology and interfirm linkages: Karanggeneng since 1988

Traditional technology was the only production technique in the cluster for decades. Skills were transmitted locally through the family. There are reports of producers that went bankrupt, but also of others that have emerged as new producers. However there were no substantial changes in the organization of production and marketing. Profits from tiles were hardly ever reinvested in the cluster. There seemed to be a shortage of interesting investment opportunities in tiles under the traditional technology regime. It has been reported elsewhere (Lestariyo and Sandee, 1989) that the semi-urban context of Karanggeneng offered a wide range of rewarding possibilities for investments in non-agricultural income-generating activities. Diversification of sources of income, rather than concentration on tiles, was an important characteristic of successful tile producers.

The handpress technology is increasingly replacing traditional production techniques in Karanggeneng since 1988. Introduction of the handpress technology leads to production of more expensive tiles of better quality for another market segment. There are a number of types of pressed tiles dependent on the type of mould. These tiles are part of another package of roofing materials for better houses for households that could afford higher construction costs. Its introduction has made a new range of sector-specific investment opportunities available to local producers which, to an important extent, have replaced opportunities elsewhere. In principle, the handpress technology does not significantly differ from the traditional way of producing tiles in the village. Tables 6.1 and 6.3 summarize some of its characteristics. Main differences concern the introduction of two complementary pieces of equipment: a hand-operated press and a mixer. Tiles are no longer printed with wooden moulds. A hand-operated press is used for printing, and this results in an improved product which is heavier, but lasts longer. However, printing with a press can only be carried out when clay is better mixed beforehand than under traditional circumstances. This requires the introduction of a power-driven mixer which supplies a mixture of clay, sand, and some fats, resulting in heavier printed tiles which do not break during firing.

There is an increased daily output from printing, which implies that a batch of 5000 tiles is produced in ten instead of fifteen days. Consequently, the frequency of firing increases. Introduction of just one press does generally not yet lead to the employment of steady wage workers, but additional presses cannot be purchased without recruitment of paid labour. The increased daily output of printed tiles has introduced the use of racks to compensate for the lack of space for drying tiles on the ground surrounding the production site. A striking difference concerns the increase in value added per family labour hour. Adoption of one press leads to an increase of the number of hours which a family has to spend in tiles production. There are many cases where adoption has forced families to cut their involvement outside tiles.

Adoption can be considered, on the one hand, as a result of growing demand from middle income consumers in the Boyolali regency and surroundings for better housing, which included the use of improved materials for roofing. It made it increasingly plausible that pressed tiles were no longer 'imported' from elsewhere, since they could be made locally. On the other hand, adoption was stimulated by the producers (suppliers) of capital goods once they discovered the attempts in Karanggeneng to change, and became aware of the local capabilities to successfully adopt. Traders in Karanggeneng were however very reluctant to support adoption. In 1988, traders were only interested in buying traditional tiles in Karanggeneng and ordered their pressed tiles in the nearby Klaten region. They were not interested in allowing Karanggeneng producers to gain a foothold in both market segments. Consequently, early adopters in Karanggeneng were forced to sell directly to consumers and had to promote their new products themselves. At that stage, there were no formal institutions and NGOs offering support.

The introduction of the press could be incorporated into the individual small enterprises replacing the traditional moulds. It concerns an investment of some 600,000 Rupiah which early adopters paid themselves, but it occasionally occurred that credit from capital goods suppliers facilitated the purchase. On the contrary, purchase of the mixer presents a very different case. In the first place, the mixer costs 2.5 million Rupiah which constitutes a high investment risk in case of adoption failure. In the second place, the capacity of the mixer is such that a total of seven producers, each using one press, can be supplied with prepared clay for press printing. Consequently collective action and interdependent decisionmaking were needed to allow for successful adoption of the complete package of intermediate technology, and also to make sure that new output could be

Table 6.3 Labour use, costs, and value added (Rupiah) of presses' tile production in Karanggeneng, 1989 (use of one press and making basic press tiles)

5000 tiles (3% breaks during firing) sales 4850 × Rp45		202 250
Length of production cycle		10 days
Costs of inputs		104 250
– Clay	7 250	
– Casual labour	36 000	
– Transport	8 000	
– Sand/water	4 000	
– Firewood	35 000	
– Oil	6 000	
– Mixing clay	9 000	
Casual labour for firing		5 000
Maintenance and repair		5 000
Value added		88 000
Value added per 1000 tiles sold		19 100
Family labour		130 hrs
Value added per family labour hour		680

Source: Own surveys, 1989 (dry season).

marketed. One forerunner paid the purchase of a mixer out of his own funds, but only after receiving assurance from others that they would, like him, buy presses and use the services of his mixer.

The first adopters were all leading firms, which in the past were mainly competing with each other, while each heading their own network. Linkages among these forerunners were mutually beneficial: orders were shared, the mixer used by all, and the new output was jointly promoted. These new networks were developed in order to aim at sustainability of the innovation. Forerunners co-operated to create themselves a supportive infrastructure, and this was necessary due to the lack of institutional support at that stage. The early adopters, however, remained the leaders of their own traditional networks for the production of traditional tiles, increasingly outcontracting part of their orders for traditional tiles to others.

Table 6.4 summarizes adoption and diffusion of the handpress technology up to June 1990. In 1989, it became clear that the handpress technology in the cluster was a success, and adopters did earn considerably more than traditional producers. The new output was of good quality, and demand was high. None of the early adopters was able to produce press tiles for stock. Many adopters decided to stop producing traditional tiles altogether. Orders were still accepted, but all jobs were outcontracted.

At this stage, the overall environment and infrastructure became much more supportive for adoption and diffusion of new technology in Karanggeneng. Suppliers of capital goods, traders, middlemen, NGOs, and also local governmental organizations have become active, and offered credit for investment on a wide variety of terms.

Table 6.4 Annual adoption of the handpress technology in Karanggeneng to June 1990: a summary

Year	Number of adopters	Average age	Sources of investments (per cent)		Number of presses
1987	1	31	Own funds	–	3
1988	4	49	Own funds	90	7
			Bank	10	
1989	12	33	Own funds	43	14
			NGO	35	
			Rental	8	
			Entrepreneur	8	
			Trader	6	
1990	15	38	Own funds	52	15
			Bank	24	
			Entrepreneur	12	
			Trader	6	
			NGO	6	

Source: Own survey in Karanggeneng, June 1990.

Suppliers of capital goods tried to contract forerunners as their local agents to promote the use of their equipment. Traders and middlemen offered credit on the strict condition that the new output would be exclusively marketed through them. NGOs were especially interested in offering cheap credit to those producers who lacked means as well as contacts. On the contrary, local government banks offered credit to early adopters, who had proven their mastery of the new technique, to expand their business. The relative importance of all these parties can be seen in Table 6.4. It concerns the acquisition of presses and not of the mixer. The table shows that many producers paid for the handpress out of their own funds.

By June 1990, four mixers were in use in Karanggeneng. Three were owned by early adopters, and another one was managed by an NGO. As explained above, mixers play a crucial role in structuring interfirm linkages and networks. Early adopters had, by June 1990, already supported their neighbours to adopt as well. The traditional networks which they controlled were transformed into 'modern' ones, concentrating on the production of press tiles. Some early adopters even decided upon the introduction of branch names printed on their own tiles and those of their subcontractors. The network managed by the NGO was different, as it was based on joint-ownership of the mixer. Shared use was the main linkage among firms, with regular conflicts as to whose needs of its services were most pressing. In this case, producers marketed their own output.

In the case where the mixer was owned by early adopters themselves, diffusion resulted in the return of traditional interfirm linkages. This allowed leading firms (early adopters) to bid for large orders. This is important since the scale of demand in the intermediate market segment is larger than in the traditional case. Here, the pattern of interfirm linkages is similar to the structure of traditional networks. However, there were also a number of developments which diverge from the traditional interfirm linkages. In the first place, within the intermediate technology market segment a distinction can be made between pressed tiles with low, medium, and high value added. There are several moulds which differ in price, and in quality and price of output. Within networks, leaders concentrate on production of high value-added products, while other forms are, if necessary, outcontracted. Generally, it concerns commercial outcontracting in the sense that the subordinate firm is responsible for the whole production cycle. In the second place, the NGO network has brought about another way of organizing production and marketing. Enterprises themselves deal with customers, and the mixer can be considered as 'merely' an additional common resource like clay and firewood. The only problem is that this new resource is very scarce, and this has caused frictions. Both networks increasingly concentrated on production and marketing of pressed tiles, and traditional tiles lost their importance.

Innovation of intermediate technology has, to an important extent, not changed the nature of interfirm linkages. New networks among leading firms (early adopters) were of a temporary nature. As soon as the indivisibilities of the new technology could be incorporated into traditional networks, co-operation between early adopters became less important. Price competition also gained more importance than in the case of traditional tiles. The new product allows for some flexibility with respect to division of tasks and orders on the basis of value added of output. Flexibility centred around the variety of moulds within a network. Different orders will lead to a different strategy of network leaders on how to incorporate others in their network. Finally, the NGO network is characterized by the fact that an outsider controls the new indivisible equipment. Here, enterprises all marketed their own output. So far, they have not run into troubles because the new tiles from Karanggeneng were in heavy demand, and none of the adopters was able to produce for stock. These enterprises were generally serving the smaller orders from final consumers, while the bigger orders were taken up by the leading enterprises and their networks.

Forecast on the pattern of further diffusion in Karanggeneng

In Karanggeneng, two patterns of interfirm linkages existed for the production of intermediate tiles, in accordance with differences in ownership patterns of mixers. What will happen next when the innovation will further diffuse among the producers in Karanggeneng? This question will be addressed here by discussing developments in two clusters where the handpress technology was introduced in the late 1970s and early 1980s. The handpress technology in these clusters was, in 1990, widely used among local enterprises, and traditional tiles production has become of very little significance.

In the cluster of Mayong, in the Jepara regency, access to mixers has become increasingly controlled by NGOs. Here, a mixer has not become an instrument for leading firms to control networks, and determine the pattern of interfirm linkages. There are no big enterprises in this cluster which dominate production and marketing. Enterprises deal often directly with final consumers and traders, and types of tiles made is an individual decision. This has limited the possibility for firms in Jepara to gain a foothold in the most dynamic part of this market segment, since big orders cannot easily be accepted by individual enterprises. Further developments in Mayong include the rise of new independent firms for repair and maintenance. In Klepu, in the Klaten regency, formal banks are very important, and have provided credit especially to early adopters. These enterprises control their own mixer, and have invested in new kilns with a capacity of 10,000–15,000 tiles. They take care of their own repair and maintenance, and some are even able to manufacture presses themselves. Leading firms are serving the 'top of the market segment'. In Klepu, interfirm linkages are now of little importance, because leading firms have incorporated most phases of the production and marketing cycle under their own roof. In both clusters, firms are occasionally confronted with lack of demand, especially in the busy rainy, agricultural season.

In both cases, the importance and pattern of interfirm linkages was strongly influenced by finance. Finance through NGOs in Mayong has contributed to networks in which tile enterprises produce and sell themselves. These enterprises do not own their own repair and maintenance facilities, nor do they market their output themselves. They fully concentrate on production, and need their network for other tasks of the production and marketing cycle. In Klepu leading firms have not only expanded horizontally, but also vertically. Horizontal expansion has led to the subordination of other firms. This had occurred both through subcontracting as well as integration. Access to formal finance has contributed to incorporation of backward and forward linkage units. Leading firms now carry out their own repair and maintenance facilities, and own trucks for transport of tiles.

Developments in Karanggeneng indicate that both patterns described above are occurring. In the first place, there are networks centred around leading firms where the division of labour and tasks among firms is a flexible one. However, the leading producers control how orders and work are distributed among linked firms, and benefits from innovation are not equally distributed. In the second place, there are networks with mixers controlled by NGOs. Here, firms have much more control over production, but have no access to the most dynamic groups of consumers. However, this had not (yet) become a serious problem due to high demand for pressed tiles from Karanggeneng. There is a tendency towards increased hierarchy of firms in most networks, but this has not stopped most firms marketing their own output whenever possible. The excess demand in Karanggeneng has allowed the various distinct patterns of interfirm linkages. Developments in Karanggeneng will not be easy to compare with either Mayong or Klepu as long as this situation of excessive demand continues.

Conclusion

Adoption of new technology may not always be tailored to integration by traditional networks and interfirm linkages. In the case of Karanggeneng this was not so much caused by technological factors, but more by economic considerations. It turned out to be too risky to adopt and diffuse the handpress technology into existing networks. Consequently, new forms of co-operation among leading firms were established, but they were of a temporary nature. Once adoption by traditional networks was considered appropriate, linkages among leading firms soon broke up.

Comparisons with other tile clusters in Central Java show that diffusion of similar technology does not necessarily follow a uniform pattern. Concentration of ownership of means of production may occur, or there may be a tendency towards widespread diffusion and equal access to production and marketing. Karanggeneng shows that, due to excess demand, yet another pattern of adoption and diffusion is possible, in which increased hierarchy in some networks coexists with a form of flexible specialization in other networks. Access and source of finance has played a major role in shaping these different patterns of interfirm linkages and networks in clusters.

7 Trade networks for flexible rural industry

HERMINE WEIJLAND

Rural industry and the quest for industrial flexibility[1]

According to recent studies on industrial organization, modern industry increasingly has to face changes in demand and technology which erode the economies of scale derived from standardization and mass production. Consequently, large enterprises in the more dynamic sectors are suffering from rigidities stemming from their established indivisibilities incorporated in their large fixed assets and ossified, one-dimensional organizations. On the other side, networks of smaller enterprises are starting up and finishing production much faster than their larger competitors (Best, 1990). Thus, after a century of industrial concentration and large-scale monopolization, the pendulum is swinging back towards fragmentation and competition.

Development literature duly has reported progress in small industry during the eighties (Anderson, 1982; UNDP, *et al.*, 1988; Levitsky, 1989; Haggblade *et al.*, 1989). All these studies report increasing profitable employment in urban small industry, but they have little faith in rural small-scale industry, which is badly documented, but supposedly stagnating due to lack of local demand and limited access to finance and technology. One may distinguish three categories of small-scale enterprises (Farbman and Lessik, 1989): (i) home-based, intermittent survival-oriented activities of individuals or a few relatives, (ii) micro enterprises with 'roughly ten or fewer full-time workers', and (iii) small-scale enterprises with ten to fifty workers. This paper analyses 'Rural Cottage Industry' (RCI hereafter), the smallest and poorest category. It intends to put this marginal category in a new light, connecting its future with the new trends in modern industrial organization. It stresses RCI's function in a flexible industrial organization, and the role middlemen play to enhance this function. The notion that RCI is increasingly connected to global industrial development struck the author at the on-site evaluation of rural industry projects in Asia. As the project data were classified, evidence for the argument had to be culled from official sources, and they were found in the census and survey statistics of rural population and cottage industry in the Indonesian provinces (BPS, 1987; 1989a; 1989b; 1989c; 1989e; World Bank, 1990).

The official survey data confirmed that Indonesia's RCI includes the world's most deprived manufacturing workers, with low literacy rates and very low incomes.[2] They are working in villages, often far away from the nearest marketplace, and hardly ever meet any of the consumers of the products they sell to their middlemen. Some fifty years ago, when development studies still emphasized modern–traditional dualism in the style of

Lewis (1954), it would have been absurd to state that such primitive enterprises could be incorporated in modern, large, complex, international production networks. However, since the advent of theories on the informal sector and petty commodity production (Moser, 1978), incorporation has become a focus of analysis, albeit that this new functional approach of traditional small enterprise has been fixed on exploitative aspects. This paper then proceeds to study the more favourable side of incorporation, contending that many poor producers might have gained by the unequal alliance with the modern sector, and even have been aided by the traditionally despised middlemen.

As the paper intends to show how RCI fits in with flexible industry, it first has to identify the special characteristics that make it a useful partner in a flexible organization.

In general, flexibility can be achieved in various ways through internal and external change:[3]

- Technological process innovation: introduction of (parts of) machinery and equipment that facilitate flexible production methods. Examples are electronic programming and steering devices;
- Increasing the variety of skills a given labour power can master (functional flexibility of labour);
- Internal re-organization: e.g. creating divisions for products or processes with cheaper or numerically more flexible labour. So, in pursuit of flexibility, large enterprises may disintegrate into multiple interlinked units or functionally separated divisions which perform better as they operate with shorter runs of output and less cost of capital and labour;
- Tapping labour power reserves outside the firm (numerical flexibility of labour);
- External organization in networks of co-operating specialized firms yielding qualitatively and/or quantitatively more flexible (and cheaper) flows of output;
- Formation of industrial districts which facilitate innovations, networking and tapping of reserves through increasing communication stemming from proximity.

Although RCI can contribute little to the upper three processes as these require large enterprises and sophisticated management, it is increasingly involved in the lower three of the list, (i) yielding a labour reserve, (ii) becoming part of industrial trade networks, and (iii) forming special types of rural industrial districts ('clusters'). The following section describes these three processes and argues that in Indonesia small traders can play a central role as initiating and stimulating middlemen. Next, the paper investigates the preconditions for the processes of flexible incorporation in Indonesia, followed by an assessment of the effects of middlemen's activities on employment and earnings in RCI.

Flexible incorporation

Flexible rural labour power and production regulations

Densely populated rural areas in Third World countries are known for their flexible labour reserves. This can be an important economic factor, especially if one considers that rural labour may not be only flexible but also very cheap. Rural areas usually are defined as dominated by agricultural production conditions. Rural villages have many non-farm RCI activities linked to the agricultural production cycle, and their production patterns are often complementary to the seasonally and daily varying activities in farming, forestry and fishing (Haggblade *et al.*, 1989). For these micro-industries not only labour but also equipment, housing and land can be shared with agrarian activities. This flexibility in resource allocation ensures optimal use, reflected by low cost of working power and capital. So agricultural seasonality favours the supply of cheap industrial labour, and indeed, since time immemorial, rural areas have served as the cheapest sources of unskilled labour for manufacturing (Oshima, 1983). Rural workers have been known to accept below-subsistence earnings in adverse times or during the slack periods of their primary employment, so they could be hired by subcontracting middlemen to do piecework in their cottages for large urban enterprises and trade houses. This was common practice in the early stages of industrialization in Europe as well as in Asia, but while the system expired in Europe, it remained operational in Asia. The oriental carpet industry is a well-known example of such a putting-out system. Similar practices have been in use in Indonesia since pre-colonial times (Alexander and Alexander, 1991), and there is evidence that they are reviving instead of fading away with the tide of modern industrial growth (White, 1992). Meanwhile, the logic of subcontracting and putting-out systems has remained the same, and the goods traded by these systems have kept the same characteristics. They are typically light consumer goods or intermediary goods, such as finished garments and materials for garments (woven, embroidered, dyed or knitted), footwear, sports articles, household utensils, small metal tools, and small products of leather, feather and wood.

Apart from flexible cheap labour and accessible raw materials, the countryside offers other attractions for manufacturing enterprises. Relocation in sparsely populated areas usually guarantees more flexible or even non-existent rules and regulations concerning labour conditions, land use and environmental damage. Thus the introduction of formal regulations on minimum age, working time and working conditions have led to ruralization and fragmentation of many industries. The tanning industry presents an example of activities which have been banned out of urban areas in most countries.

Empirical studies on a worldwide scale show that high employment rates in rural industry are often attained by high participation of women and children. Poor women tend to participate with their children in the most irregular and least gainful activities (Haggblade *et al.*, 1989). As they volunteer to work for very long hours at irregular intervals whenever money has to be paid to repair sickness or some other family crisis, they would constitute the most flexible work force in poverty-stricken areas. This hypothesis is corroborated by the official Indonesian cottage industry statistics, which show that female participation in RCI varies from some 30 per cent in the richest provinces to 60 per cent in the poorest ones (see Table 7.1 (page 107), row 15). Child labour is not recorded for obvious reasons, but even the official records of female labour are dubious, because cultural factors often hinder correct enumeration, so that in some very poor provinces the statistics of female participation are surprisingly low. In such places it is likely that convention dictates that women remain unseen and uncounted.

Having established that poor rural areas are often good suppliers of cheap flexible labour power, one may wonder why modern industry and trade has not tapped this source more consistently. One probable reason is that the very nature of RCI labour power implies that it usually lacks specialized skills and capital. So it can perform only simple tasks and produce simple goods. Simple in this sense means small product size, short production process, low degree of complexity, little precision, and no standardization. Thus far, most studies on RCI have supposed that such simple RCI goods can be sold only in small quantities in local poor markets, and that RCI therefore is bound to decline with growing rural welfare (Anderson, 1982; Haggblade *et al.*, 1989). Another reason for ignoring RCI's potential could be that it has yet another serious handicap, namely isolation. Geographic isolation incurs high cost of market incorporation, which include the cost of transport, monitoring, and technical and financial services. These costs tend to rise with distance, dispersion, smallness, and cultural discrepancies, which make the work force in isolated villages inaccessible.

Trade networks for small villages

As dispersion and isolation put such high barriers to trade, the size of villages has been found a crucial factor. Many studies on rural industry therefore distinguish between small villages and larger rural centres. In Haggblade's survey the borderline was drawn at 20,000 inhabitants (Haggblade *et al.*, 1989), and according to this classification small villages would have only some basic crafts and simple processing activities, while the larger centres have more and increasing RCI employment, concentrated in more sophisticated manufacturing activities such as metal working, furniture, textiles and footwear (ibid). So it would seem that village size is indeed a powerful determinant for rural industry, and this for various reasons. For one, larger centres would have the critical minimum scale of local demand required for full specialization in the manufacturing subsectors. Furthermore, they would have better transport facilities for export-oriented production and could offer the other infrastructural services needed for more advanced manufacturing activities. The Indonesian industrial records, however, do not always corroborate this reasoning, and show that in certain regions RCI has developed in small villages without the support of a local market. This anomaly can be explained when we consider the economic functions of middlemen. Case studies and anthropological surveys report that Indonesia's populous rural regions are covered by various trade networks which link RCI with distant markets (e.g. Alexander and Alexander, 1990 and 1991; Sandee, this volume). Such networks are typical for densely-populated areas with ancient trade cultures as can be found in many Asian countries, where trade channels often reach RCI in isolated villages, which then receive essential technical information, advances for labour, and provision of materials and equipment through middlemen.

Rural trade networks can be very wide and complex, and stretch far into the countryside, especially when they involve small traders with simple vehicles that can manage bad roads. At the lowest echelons many of these middlemen are in fact 'middlewomen', who are living in the neighbourhood of their clients and therefore are well acquainted, which enhances stable relationships and mutually benefiting transactions (Knorringa and Weijland, 1993; Rasmussen, 1992). Based on local traditions of trust and mutual dependence between traders, farmers and artisans, rural industries can develop even in small and distant villages (see Sandee, this volume). According to industrial census and survey data, an increasing part of the Indonesia's RCI is in this way connected to wider markets. Only the most isolated industries with prohibitive transaction costs have to be confined to their small local markets. Thus, less than 50 per cent of RCI is selling to local markets (Table 7.1, row 12), and this percentage is still decreasing. Urban CI, on the other hand, shows the opposite tendency with an average of 75 per cent selling in the local market (BPS, 1989a, Table 10.2). Urban cottage industry need not be so export-oriented as it has better local alternatives. With a sufficiently wide local market, small urban enterprises obviously prefer to produce non-tradable, personal goods or services that are fitted to local tastes and personal producer-client contacts. Such branches yield more stable and fairer incomes. Rural workers, however, do not have such good market niches, and must be continually on the look-out for the less stable jobs offered by passing traders or local middlemen.

Clustering

In addition to establishing relations with trade networks, rural workers in Indonesia since time immemorial have found another remedy for their isolation and corresponding scale and transaction cost problems by clustering. Of the total of 67,979 Indonesian villages (BPS, 1989d), some 10,000 have been identified as industrial clusters.[4] Especially if their markets are extended beyond the direct environment, small cottage industry tends to flock hamlet-wise in groups of some 10 to 100 more or less individually-operating workers and family enterprises, producing mostly for traders, subcontractors or small middlemen. Clustering does not necessarily imply co-operation. In the most primitive clusters where technology is limited to rudimentary equipment, workers may not find any technical reason for collaboration, and so keep operating independently, without sharing labour, housing or equipment. But even in such primitive clusters the external agglomeration economies may be substantial, for the proximity of similar enterprises facilitates information sharing and innovation, and also attracts traders and suppliers of materials and equipment. These agglomeration effects broaden and intensify with the advent of more advanced technology with more indivisibility aspects, giving ample technical reasons and opportunities to collaborate by hiring each other's labour and equipment, subcontracting work from each other and selling each other's products. Thus the more developed clusters may form densely structured organizations with frequent contacts and tight social control. Through co-operative organization, cluster members can obtain capital, raw materials and services that otherwise would remain inaccessible. In this way the indivisibility problems that are conventionally associated with small enterprise can be overcome, and through this 'collective efficiency' RCI can become more viable and competitive (Best, 1990; Schmitz, 1989).

Clustering may lead to specialization of entire villages (Smyth, 1990), and it can extend to all kinds of linked activities. Large specialized villages offer considerable transaction cost reductions to the various subcontractors and trading middlemen as the clusters' inhabitants still tend to observe the village norms and values, so that transaction risks and monitoring cost are relatively low. Another advantage is that they offer better choice in product quantity and quality. But specialization can be dangerous as it makes the villagers too vulnerable to market fluctuations, and therefore one often finds that most RCI workers and craftsmen still have some secondary source of income that can safeguard survival (Sandee and Weijland, 1989).

Enabling environment for regional incorporation

In the previous sections we have argued that RCI can be linked to wider industrial systems, and that in Indonesia this incorporation process is well on its way. But the international literature on rural industry suggests that outward orientation of rural industry is not so common in Third World countries, and also in Indonesia it does not occur everywhere. The Indonesian archipelago includes thousands of islands with a wide variety of economical, cultural and natural endowments, creating such different entrepreneurial milieus for rural industry that RCI abounds in some provinces while it is almost absent in others. So there are conditions that favour or hamper outward orientation. In the standard literature on small-scale industry it has become common practice to distinguish between demand pull and supply push factors determining RCI development (UNDP *et al.*, 1988). Demand pull factors include increasing incomes of existing markets, decreasing relative RCI prices and consequent increasing demand, and geographical extension of markets. So demand factors include phenomena that manifest themselves on various levels, ranging from international to local, such as general macro developments (e.g. growth of national and regional income), and policies that raise the country's export potential (e.g. devaluation), policies that favour labour intensive industry (e.g. higher interest rates and higher prices for machinery), and policies that favour small industry (e.g. non-discriminatory credit policies). Within an unfavourable macro environment RCI cannot compete in wider markets and consequently it will stagnate (Stewart and Ranis, 1990). Like in other countries, the macro context for RCI has improved considerably in Indonesia since the introduction of more liberal trade policies. Unfortunately, this cannot be demonstrated in the empirical part of this paper, as it is limited to cross-section analysis at a single point of time. So the general macro context is given only a modest role, being represented by variations in provincial product. The study is better suited to highlight the effects of various local demand pull and supply push conditions of RCI, and differences in entrepreneurial environment.

Local demand pull factors have been given much emphasis in the literature on rural industry. This is consistent with the standard assumption that it is a primarily inward-oriented activity, located mostly in the larger rural centres where it serves mainly local rural households and enterprises. RCI's prospects then are related to the development of forward and backward linkages with other rural activities (Ranis, 1990). The latter linkages are associated with agricultural prosperity and rural equality (UNDP *et al.*, 1988; Ranis, 1990). But we have argued before that the local markets in the countryside often are too small for the sustenance of RCI, and in that case agricultural prosperity would not have the supporting effect emphasized in the aforementioned studies. To the contrary, it could imply that agriculture and other primary activities would offer better employment opportunities than RCI could, or that the village workers would be drawn to the nearby larger centres to establish larger enterprises or find better jobs (UNDP *et al.*, 1988). In that case we are left with local supply push and entrepreneurial milieu to explain the existence and further outward development of RCI. Local supply push factors would include low agricultural incomes stemming from land fragmentation, low productivity, and high poverty incidence, which would represent the push factors for non-farm activities. Such activities would be stimulated in a favourable entrepreneurial milieu, implying proximity of large

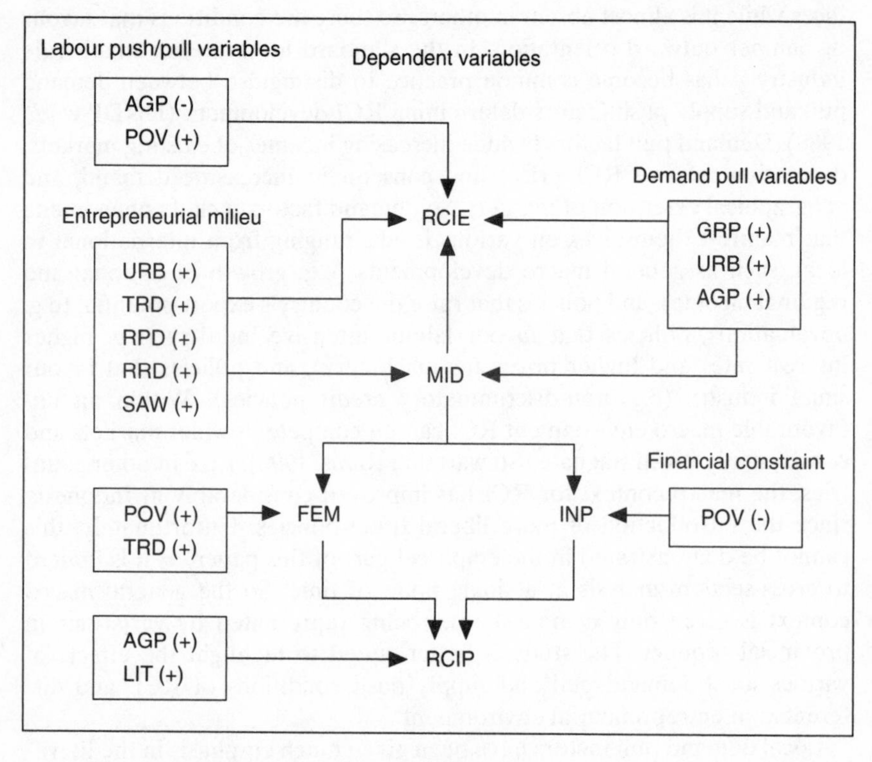

Figure 7.1 *Model of RCI and middlemen*

urban market outlets, the existence of trade networks, high rural population density, and adequate rural infrastructure (UNDP *et al.*, 1988; Rasmussen, 1992). In Indonesia the prevalence of the wet rice system would be another milieu indicator proxying traditional rural organization, which can be associated with social control, stability, and, consequently, low transaction costs.

In an analytical model the above mentioned factors would account for RCI employment intensity, defined as the total of enumerated RCI workers as a percentage of rural economic active population, corrected for the part of total work hours in RCI. As the paper intends to highlight the outward orientation of RCI and the function of middlemen, something more should be said about RCI's marketing practices, the use of middlemen services, and RCI earnings. The argument then runs as follows. It is assumed (and empirically verified) that middlemen connections are the more easily found the more traders are living in the countryside. Moreover, it is verified that, in a traditional Asian environment, middlemen services are needed more by poor women than by poor men. Consequently, easy access to middlemen would raise female participation, but as the rural female workers are found to be more illiterate and poor, they are assumed to purchase less inputs, which would depress their earnings. But it also has been argued that an important middleman function would be to provide for information and inputs. So, on the one hand, middlemen can be assumed to raise RCI employment by drawing poorer labour categories into RCI, which could have a negative effect on RCI productivity, but on the other hand this effect might be compensated by provision of information and inputs.

Aside from these complex interactions, yet another, more traditional economic determinant for RCI productivity and earnings has to be taken into account, namely the alternative earnings in larger scale enterprises and other competing rural activities, such as agriculture. As was mentioned before, prosperous agriculture would pull the marginal workers from RCI towards agriculture, and this exodus would lead to a rise in the productivity of the remaining more viable RCI.

The quantifiable variables and relationships, shown schematically in Figure 7.1, are therefore:

- RCI employment (RCIE)
- RCI productivity (RCIP)
- Female participation (FEM)
- Inputs value per worker (INP)
- Percentage of enterprises using middlemen (MID)

RCI employment determinants (with assumed signs):

○ Macro demand pull variable:	High gross regional product per worker (GRP+)
○ Local demand pull variable:	High agricultural product per worker (AGP+)
○ Local supply push variables:	Low agricultural product per worker (AGP–) High poverty incidence (POV+)
○ Entrepreneurial milieu:	Urbanization degree (URB+) Rural traders per economically active (TRD+) Rural population density (RPD+) Sawah land proportion (SAW+)
○ Productivity determinants:	Literacy rate of RCI workers (LIT+) Value of inputs per worker (INP+) Agricultural productivity (AGR+)
○ Inputs determinants:	Poverty incidence (POV–)

Use of middlemen services (MID+)

- Female participation determinants: Poverty incidence (POV+)
  Access to traders (TRD+)

Regional incorporation patterns in Indonesia

In order to demonstrate regional differentiation of trade incorporation of RCI in Indonesia, regional data are presented in Table 7.1. RCI data were taken from the industrial census and two subsequent cottage industry surveys from 1986–87, which give data on labour, output, inputs, marketing and finance of the enterprises.[5] The above hypothesized tendencies have been verified cross-section-wise with provincial data (Weijland, 1991). Here we present a general picture of the tendencies for four regions grouped according to criteria that correspond with the variables found essential for RCI development, namely population density, trade networks, agrarian system, and resource endowment (UNDP *et al.*, 1988; Haggblade *et al.*, 1989).[6] Thus we have the following regions:

- Densely-populated centre provinces (DPCP): Java (West[7], Central, and East Java, Yogyakarta); Bali;
- Settled outer island provinces (SOIP): part of Sumatra (North, West and South Sumatra, and Lampung); part of Sulawesi (North and South Sulawesi); South Kalimantan;
- Resource-rich provinces (RRP): the remaining part of Sumatra (Aceh, Bengkulu, Jambi, Riau); part of Kalimantan (West, East and Central); Irian Jaya;
- Isolated provinces (IP): Nusa Tenggara (East and West); the remaining part of Sulawesi (Central and South-East); Maluku.

With a rural economic active population of 30 millions (ACT, row 4), the DPC provinces represent densely-populated rural areas with almost 300 persons per km^2 (RPD, row 7) and an ancient agrarian organization (*sawah* irrigation, SAW, row 8), which favoured trade employment (TRD, row 6) and traditional rural industry (RCIE, row 5). The settled outer island provinces, with a total of ten million rural workers, have population densities averaging at only one-tenth of those in the centre. But they have similar agrarian systems and industry and trade traditions. The resource-rich provinces, on the other hand, have very low rural population densities and little industrial tradition, but naturally they are favoured by their manifestly abundant resources, which even when oil is excluded, is boosting their regional products and urbanization (rows 1, 2 and 3). Only the isolated provinces, consisting of small isolated and mountainous island economies, are lacking in all possible favourable conditions for RCI. So DPCP scores highest with its favourable preconditions, SOIP and RRP are in a medium

Table 7.1 Rural cottage industry and its environment in Indonesia, 1986

	DPCP	SOIP	RRP	IP
Regional indicators				
1. GRP (Gross regional product per ACT) (000Rp)	1180	1353	1694	964
2. AGP (Agricultural product per ACT) (000Rp)	606	753	944	598
3. URB (Urbanization rate) (%)	21	19	18	10
Rural employment				
4. ACT (Rural economy active population) (000)	29277	9648	4153	3447
5. RCIE (Rural cottage industry employment) (% of ACT)				
6. TRD (Trade employment) (% of ACT)				
Rural milieu				
7. RPD (Rural population density per km²)	281	29	9	20
8. SAW (Wet rice land) (%)				
9. POV (Poverty incidence) (%)				
Cottage industry characteristics				
10. RCIP (RCI value added per ACT) (000Rp)	332	508	610	401
11. INP (Inputs per establishment per year) (000Rp)	1329	1888	1508	900
12. DIR (Direct sales to consumer) (%)	27	29	42	57
13. MID (Use of middlemen) (%)	40	36	25	22
14. LIT (Literacy of entrepreneurs) (%)	36	56	52	48
15. FEM (Female participation) (%)	48	42	27	35

Data sources

GRP Gross product (excluding oil) per worker by province, 1986. BPS, 1989e:90–124; BPS, 1987:338
AGP Agricultural product per worker, 1986. BPS, 1989e:90–124; BPS, 1987:338
URB Urban population percentage of total, 1985, BPS, 1987
ACT Rural active population, 1985, BPS, 1987:335
RCIE Rural cottage industry employment, 1986 (%ACT), BPS, 1989a:48; 1987:333
TRD Workers in wholesale and retail trade, 1985, BPS, 1987:333
RPD Rural population density. Population statistics, 1985, excluding townships
SAW Wetland area as percentage of cultivated land, 1986, BPS, 1989d:210–11
POV Rural poverty incidence 1980, percentages, Hill, 1989:42–43
RCIP Cottage industry value added per worker, 1986 and 1987 (000Rp) BPS, 1989a:149, 111; BPS, 1989b:134
INP Intermediate inputs per cottage establishment per year, 1986 and 1987 (000Rp), BPS, 1989a:148; BPS, 1989b:146
DIR Percentage of RCI units selling directly to consumers, BPS, 1989b:113
MID Percentage of RCI units selling to middlemen 1986, BPS, 1989a:102; BPS, 1989b:110
LIT Literacy rate of RCI workers, BPS, 1989b:29
FEM Female participants in RCI, BPS 1986, 1989a:108

position, while IP scores lowest. It would follow that RCI employment as a percentage of rural active population would be highest in the centre and lowest in the isolated provinces, but this is not supported by the statistics of RCIE, showing first an expected fall from 6.5 per cent RCIE in DPCP to 4.0 per cent in SOPI and 2.3 in RRP, but then a rise again to 4.5 per cent in IP (row 5). The latter rise can be due only to rural poverty, which has pushed poor workers and especially poor women towards some home industry.[8] The rural people in IP are very poor by any standard – whether regional product (GRP, row 1), farm income (ACP, row 2) or poverty incidence (POV, row 9), so that the push towards cottage industry employment is high in spite of unfavourable market conditions.

Indications for market access are offered by the rural trading population (TRD, row 6) and the part of RCI enterprises using middlemen services (MID, row 13). MID shows a consistently declining trend, from 40 per cent for DPCP, 36 for SOIP, 25 for RRP, to 22 for IP. So the use of middlemen services tend to correspond more with the demand pull factors for RCI than with RCI's need for employment. The obvious conclusion would be that in places like IP, where enabling environment is lacking, cottage industry is driven by local labour supply and poor local markets only. This tendency can be further demonstrated by the consistent increase of the share of output marketed directly to local consumers as the aforementioned favourable conditions are decreasing (DIR, row 12). The IP situation differs structurally from that in the centre, where excessive supply of labour may be equally evident, but where trade networks are dense (TRD, row 6), and middlemen very active. The table shows that 11.9 per cent of the rural population is active in trade in DPCP, whereas this percentage falls to 6.2 in IP. Doubtlessly trading in the centre is stimulated by low transaction and transport cost, associated with high rural population density. In addition, DPCP enterprises can exploit cheap labour because of high rural poverty incidence (POV, 32.6 per cent, row 9). Moreover, the centre has a vast reservoir of dependent women workers with the lowest rate of literacy (rows 14 and 15). All this results in high RCI employment with low earnings in DPCP, falling to Rp 332,000 value added per worker per year, or less than a dollar a day (RCIP, row 10). So it turns out that 'favourable conditions' do not necessarily imply high earnings for RCI. They even do not imply easy access, for in spite of their more accessible markets, poor workers find it hard to respond to market opportunities as they can purchase hardly any inputs (INP, column 11) and therefore create correspondingly small added values. Their only luck is that, under certain conditions, middlemen can solve some of their financial problems. The trade sector in general and middlemen in particular appear to abound in the centre. About 40 per cent of the RCI enterprises in the centre use middlemen, while only 27 per cent sell directly to local customers.

The settled outer island provinces present an interesting case. Here rural population density is much lower than in the centre, so one might expect less RCI potential. However, the SOIP people are less poor, and their higher regional productivities would imply stronger demand pull forces. But they also could imply better alternative employment opportunities and consequently less supply of the lower labour categories. And indeed, compared to the centre, RCI employment is lower (4 per cent, row 5). According to other sources it is also less specialized and provides less primary incomes (BPS, 1989a). But the higher incomes for the RCI workers allow for more purchased inputs (INP, row 11), which contribute to higher RCI earnings. It is noteworthy that even under these favourable circumstances RCI still tends to sell more to traders than to local customers.

Compared with SOIP, the resource-rich provinces with higher incomes theoretically should offer even better opportunities for RCI. It is clear, however, that the regional demand pull factors, GRP and AGP, have no visible positive influence on total RCIE. To the contrary, they apparently depress RCIE, presumably through offering better employment opportunities outside RCI. And considering population densities around five persons per km^2, traders will soon find it unattractive to visit the interior, so RCI would have to orient itself more to its local market. But low population density narrows the local markets, and consequently RCIE falls to some 2 per cent (row 5). However, it is rather prosperous compared to RCIE in the other regions, and with low poverty incidence and low female participation, middlemen services seem to be less needed.

The isolated provinces, finally, give the most dismal picture. Isolation may hinder competition, but it also prohibits marketing, and with very small local markets the marketing problems are most serious. Given the long distances it is not plausible that middlemen can be very active here, and the statistics show that direct selling in the poor local markets remains predominant in IP.

Conclusion

RCI in Indonesia has been shown to depend heavily on wider market networks and middlemen who help to make these accessible. Its prospects seem to be limited in isolated regions with few natural resources. Such places do not attract traders, so RCI remains a poverty-driven activity bound to decline when other sources of income are offered. In regions with relatively abundant resources a typically resource-based industry can develop if access to distant markets can be gained and communication channels improved. Densely-populated areas with good trade networks are probably the most favourable seedbeds for rural industry.

Statistical analysis[9] suggests that a substantial and increasing part of employment and income in RCI would be related only indirectly to local economic growth, as RCI appears to depend primarily on intermediaries for the marketing of outputs and financing of inputs. Policy implications would be that demand-oriented policies of a macro nature might not suffice for the very small enterprises, as they would need additional measures to remedy their weak financial position and poor access to markets. These findings as such are not new, but the data on middlemen suggest that, in addition to the conventional policies of a macro and micro nature, regional policies addressing subcontracting producers and traders might deserve consideration as a special instrument to reach the poorest rural workers.

8 Weaving flexibility: Large–small firm relations, flexibility and regional clusters in South Korea

MYUNG-RAE CHO

Since the mid-1980s, South Korea's industrial system has been subject to an immense pressure in its restructuring towards a technologically competitive regime of production. Diverse social actors, orchestrated by the state, are involved in creating new social dynamics for re-industrialization. In the social organization of the new economy, a new type of interfirm relations appear to be highly effective in overcoming technological, financial and marketing problems.

A central aspect of this process is the reconfiguration of relationships between large and small firms. This is because of the domination of a handful of conglomerates in the national economy. However, as microelectronic-based process technology spreads, new production relations tend to become more flexible. This flexibility is generated mainly by the sectoral and spatial clustering of new interfirm networks woven around technically interconnected production processes.

Against this background, this study seeks to explore the form and function of new interfirm relations which create the basis of a flexible production system. Focusing on large–small firm relations, the study analyses three types of regional clusters of corporate networks. At the micro level the emphasis is on unravelling the mechanisms conducive to flexibility and collective efficiency. In so doing, the study is implicitly addressed to a critical examination of the theoretical validity of the flexible specialization thesis for countries like Korea.

New facets of Korea's industrial development

A shift towards high technology industrial development

In South Korea (hereafter, Korea), fully-fledged capitalist industrial development commenced with the rise of a military government led by General Park in 1961. Since then, Korea's industrial development has grown at an unprecedented rate. In spite of its short history, however, Korean development can be said to have undergone three distinct phases (see Cho, 1991a).

The first phase falls between 1961 and 1972. During this period, the role of manufacture in the national economy was increased at the expense of agriculture. Simultaneously, as an export-oriented strategy was gradually adopted, emerging manufacturing activities focused on the production of labour-intensive, exportable, consumer goods such as textiles and shoes.

However, the lack of an integrated and complete industrial structure also made itself felt during this period.

The second stage began with the launching of a large-scale heavy and chemical industrialization project by President Park, in conjunction with the formation of a bureaucratic authoritarian regime in 1973. The major effort of the state was devoted to the structuring of capital-labour relations in strategic industries like steel, shipbuilding and heavy chemicals. It was during this period that the core of the Korean economy was solidly founded on a modern manufacturing system and, more importantly, that a number of conglomerate business groups called *Chaebol* were formed. However, because of heavy dependency on foreign sources of capital, technology and market, new capital-intensive activities were only remotely related to the traditional and endogenous sector of economy. Lacking in integration and autonomy, this structure was therefore susceptible to crisis due to global economic fluctuations.

The third phase set in by the mid-1980s, aiming at a shift towards high technology industrialization. The forces behind this were, on the one hand union struggles, which increased the price of labour; on the other hand the opportunity for entering production of technically competitive, cheap consumer goods.

The new wave of industrial expansion was spearheaded by electrics/electronics, precision machine tools and transport equipment. When high technology like electronics, mechatronics and precision chemicals swept through Korea's industrial production system, an extensive industrial restructuring took place. The emergent industrial relations were simultaneously characterized by increased integration and more flexibility.

Flexible interfirm relations

The 1987 labour unrest brought about the strengthening of bargaining power leading to a rapid rise in wages. The average real wage index soared to 219.3 in 1990, as compared to 113.6 for the U.S, 116.3 for Japan and 174.6 for Taiwan (1985=100). This process changed customer's tastes, as basic needs were satisfied and possibilities created for the purchasing of consumer durables. Externally, tougher price and quality competition in world markets as well as strong international pressure for the opening of domestic Korean markets to competitive foreign commodities made imperative the upgrading of Korean products.

Volatile and diversified demand induces a flexible response from producers. Yet, this motive tends to be mixed with the desire to bring labour processes under more flexible capitalist control. The result is reorganization of production, undertaken in all industrial sectors, as indicated by the rapid diffusion of so-called 'flexible manufacturing systems'.

Organization of the complex input-output network of production, distribution and marketing requires flexible synchronization of material and informational flows among the units involved in the new social division of labour. Because firms are key actors in creating them, such networks mainly take the form of interfirm co-operation, alliance, affiliation, subcontracting and the like (Sayer and Walker, 1992). The Korean model of interfirm networks must be understood with a point of departure in large–small firm relations, chiefly because of the domination of a handful of conglomerates in the national economy. This compels small firms to become either dependent on or functionally affiliated to large firms. However, as large firms branch into new industries such as automobiles and microelectronics, large–small firm relationships develop into organic and flexible networks in which large firms depend on small firms to perform specific tasks.

These large–small firm networks facilitate sharing of specialized competence between large and small firms, such as the technology, innovative capacity, financing and market outlets of large firms, and the niche-based technical skills, diversification capability and flexible labour/wage relations in small firms.

Large–small firm relations usually take the form of subcontracting. The share of small subcontracting firms in manufacture expanded from 30 per cent in 1980 to 59.1 per cent in 1988. In 1988, 75 per cent of small firms in the metal assembly and machinery equipment sector were subcontracting firms, 82.9 per cent in electrics/electronics and 80.5 per cent in transport equipment. In all industries, 80 per cent of all small firms produced over 80 per cent of their value added under subcontracting contracts in 1988. In 1991, it was reported that 1100 large lead firms had various supply-demand relations with 12,500 small firms and 102 branch associations or councils dealt with collaboration and co-operation among these firms.

Techno-spatial clustering

A central driving force of recent industrial restructuring evolves out of technical and organizational changes in the large firms affiliated to conglomerate business groups, that is the *Chaebol*. From the early 1980s onwards, most conglomerates have tried to increase the share of high technology industries. Among the internal measures undertaken to this end, the most comprehensive is the so-called 'systematization of enterprises' which means the combining of existing firms in a mutually connected line of business via mergers or re-setup, into a production regime especially tailored to hi-tech commodities.

When leading enterprises move up the technological ladder, their associated or even remotely related small-scale businesses are forced to follow suit. Hence, the central emphasis of the industrial system has changed, from labour-intensive industry (typically textiles) of the sixties, through the heavy and chemical industry (typically machines and chemicals) of the seventies, to the high-technology industries (typically electronics) of the eighties.

This shift has involved the restructuring of the entire industrial system. In fact, the industrial restructuring under way since the mid-1980s affected all three techno-industrial subsystems:

- o the promotion of new high technology industries like micro-electronics and mechatronics;
- o the expansion of capital-intensive mature industries like motor-vehicles;
- o the rationalization of traditionally labour-intensive industries like textiles. (Cho, 1991b)

Each of the three subsystems corresponds to the upper, middle and lower levels of the technological hierarchy of Korea's current industrial system.

Further, as large firms produce new commodities composed of numerous parts or components (notably machine assembly and transport equipment), small firms are subcontracted to supply those parts and components. This situation has created a plethora of new small firms, most of which are, in one way or another, integrated into the new hi-tech production circuit dominated by large firms.

In 1990, more than 60 per cent of all existing enterprise were ten years old or less. Given that large firms are only 1 per cent of these, practically all new firms fall under the category of small (and medium) enterprise. Most of these new firms are in the metal assembly, machinery equipment and industrial chemicals sectors.

As implied earlier, the production of new products in large firms runs through complicated and fragmented processes which demand not only a re-demarcation of jobs along technical lines within a firm, but also increased externalization and specialization among firms. In general the trend is towards a deepening of social division of labour, from intrafirm specialization to externalization and interfirm specialization.

The ways in which production in large and small firms is integrated varies across industrial sectors. This is largely because each (sub)sector has different technological, locational, labour and market prerequisites. These industrial and geographical conditions have created clusters of interfirm relations which are sectorial as well as spatially distinct. The industrial changes since the mid-1980s have therefore created three archetypal techno-spatial clusters which are brought together to shape the techno-spatial complex of Korea's new industrial system:

- o Seoul region for high technology like micro-electronics;
- o Ulsan for middle technology like motor-vehicles;
- o Daegu for lower technology like textiles.

In what follows, each of the three clusters is analysed in detail.

Three regional clusters

Micro-electronics and Seoul metropolitan region

Since the beginning of the 1980s, the possibility of high technology industries has been explored, on the initiative of large firms and mainly around the Seoul metropolitan region. Today about 81 per cent of hi-tech industrial plants are located in this region (Park, 1991). This is the rule in particular in microelectronics. This is shown by the fact that in 1989, 86.4 per cent of semiconductors, computers and software were produced in this region.

Korea's electronics started with the labour-intensive assembly of imported parts by using cheap female labour. But, thanks to massive investment directed by the government and private conglomerates firms, this sector has ascended to the third position in the world, only behind Japan and the USA. Today, microelectronic technology permeates all branches of industry, and mechatronics such as NC, CNC, CIM, CAD and robots have emerged as the most promising high technology industries.

The microelectronics industries are dominated by the large conglomerates which encompass a vertically integrated network linking closely R&D, parts supply, assembly and marketing. A typical case is Lucky Gold Star Group, the third largest conglomerate business group in Korea. Twenty-three of the forty-eight firms of this group are in electronics and produce virtually the whole spectrum of electronic goods from semiconductors, computers, TV sets, audio and telephone equipment to software, robots, and aerospace equipment. Each firm operates its own internal division of labour according to Taylorist principles. The top level in the hierarchy is design and operations management, the middle level is skilled machine manufacturing and the bottom level is unskilled execution.

In the conglomerate structure, however, the intrafirm division of labour is attuned to the extended interfirm network. The units of an individual firm apparently operate within an independent corporate organization, but their technological, financial and commercial activities are tied together by the managerial circuit of the conglomerate. This has created a socio-spatial division of labour, in which the upper functions like R&D tend to be concentrated in the metropolitan region, with the lower functions such as assembly and unskilled execution in peripheral regions.

Among the Lucky Gold Star Group units in the Seoul metropolitan region are, to name but a few, Gold Star Central Research Institute, Gold Semiconductor Co., Gold Star Industrial Electronic Co. and Gold Star Machinery and Electronic Co. Major products of these firms are telecommunication equipment, precision machinery, aerospace, robots, FMS and the like. Within the technical division of labour on a group scale, most of these firms operate at the level of highly innovative technologies.

The internal channels of the group regulate strongly the sharing of finance, know-how, machinery, materials and sale outlets among them.

Externally, they often seek to build a strategic alliance with foreign technical firms (mainly from Japan), university or government-run research institutes and, in some cases, other conglomerates. Through these alliances, they intend not only to acquire innovative technology, know-how and hi-tech components, but also to keep domestic hi-tech commodity markets under their monopolistic control. This kind of alliance is often politically protected and closed to outsiders.

In the actual production sphere, most plants have been extensively reorganized, particularly after the nation-wide labour unrest of 1987. Major production lines are now equipped with varied flexible manufacturing systems such as CNC.

As regards interfirm relations, there are two essential features of the reorganization. One is the reshaping of existing Taylorist labour processes through innovative technical enrichment, job re-demarcation and rearrangement. The other is the externalization of production processes which are either sensitive to labour cost and disruption, or dependent on technical contributions from other firms.

In these changes, the fabric of interfirm relations is woven most thickly and this is especially noticeable in the sector of electronic assembly such as computer, video and audio. Not only is the technical know-how created through the strategic alliances discussed above translated and applied to the practical organization of production. The specialized competence of a myriad of small firms is also incarnated in the final products.

The contracting relationships in microelectronics are, by and large, mediated by collaborative associations with large lead firms form with hundreds of small firms. For Lucky Gold Star Business Group, the association named *Seong-Ryuk-Hoe* (Star Power Association) plays a critical role in accommodating and administering subcontracting affairs in all business branches of the group. The sections of the Association increased in number from 52 in 1983 to 183 in 1988. A 1989 survey of a Gold Star video assembly plant in Seoul found that this plant has diverse types of subcontracting relationships with 223 small firms and 87.2 per cent of these are located in the Seoul metropolitan area. Fifty-one are members of the Association (Lee, 1989).

The main function of the associations is securing the interests of small firms on the basis of contracts assuming legal equality of the parties. The operation of a high technology production system forces large firms to grant this status to small subcontracting firms, because small firms produce specialized goods and services that large firms cannot make equally efficiently in-house.

Improvement in the technical capacity of small supplier firms has been considerable, due to a variety of technical and financial assistance that large firms extend to them (in line with the new act of small firm promotion). As the role of small firms is upgraded, large–small firm relationships become more associational and collaborative in nature, although much of their hierarchical character remains. Small firms, each contributing its particular speciality, are therefore increasingly forming quasi-horizontal networks clustered around the core of large lead firms.

However, the limbs of microelectronic production reach down hierarchical layers of subcontracting, all the way to workplaces where piecework is carried out by hundreds of thousands of housewives or the elderly for low wages. Their tasks, such as wrapping various sizes of inductors with coils, constitute the lower segment of labour intensive production which is put out by subcontracting small firms. In this way they are, via a complex subnetwork of small firm production relations, functionally integrated into a hi-tech production regime led by conglomerate firms.

Recapitulating, the metropolitan network of micro-electronics production consists of a few innovative technological nuclei, diversified niche skills, an abundant labour force, flexible parts/material supply and widespread outlets. A key aspect of the network is the large–small firm relations through which a myriad of production and service activities, ranging from conglomerates' R&D to housewives' piecework, are woven into a dense and flexible network for microelectronics production. As a whole, Seoul metropolitan region can be characterized as a *system area* which Leborgne and Lipietz (1988) define as a cluster of regionally integrated, diversified, multi-sectoral networks; the locus of multi-regional firms, incubator of new hi-tech firms, and a site of technological innovation.

The economic logic of such networks can be understood in the light of the economies of scope which occur 'where it is more efficient to operate two activities in tandem than each in isolation' (Dunford, 1991). On the other hand, the economies of scope have some similarity to co-operation or system economies in that integration of labour processes and regulation of material flows can benefit overall production. Examples of this are close links between R&D and manufacturing or joint marketing of a line of products.

Such economies of scope in microelectronics production are greatly facilitated by the complex and flexible networks of the metropolitan region. Through these networks, innovative technology diffuses from the upper to the lower tier of technological firms, individual creativity is translated into collective innovation, and interaction among actors creates complementarities. The networking between core, large, innovative firms and small technical firms is particularly conducive to the realization of innovation by collective efforts.

Automobiles and Ulsan industrial town

Korea's modern automobile industry was initiated in the mid-sixties. Since then several domestic conglomerates have strived to set up new, lucrative businesses through strategic alliances with multinationals in pursuit of political favour. In contrast to the internal production capability of large firms, the industry-wide supporting basis, such as sophisticated technology, suppliers of requisite parts and skilled manpower, has been poorly established. Despite these adverse conditions, the total production capacity of Korea's three major motorvehicle concerns reached one million cars per annum in 1986. The next year the automobile industry was hit by sweeping industrial disputes and the technical backwardness of automobile industry suddenly became a burning question.

The reorganization of automobile production was accomplished by two means. One is the enhancement of the technical flexibility of internal production processes by introducing a multitude of computer-controlled machines. This internal change ushered in the set-up of new specialized technical divisions or firms whose operation in turn requires a new type of skilled labour. The other is the externalization of many production segments into competent small firms with niche-based labour force and know-how. Both internal and external changes have reinforced each other and this has been facilitated by their spatial clustering. The most outstanding instance of this is Hyundae Automobile Industrial Co. in Ulsan in the south-eastern province.

Ulsan is Korea's first and largest industrial town comprising four distinct large heavy and chemical industrial complexes and producing almost 30 per cent of the national manufacturing output. Ulsan's industrial heart consists of 23 gigantic firms affiliated to Korea's largest conglomerate, Hyundae Business Group. Included in the Group are, notably, Hyundae Heavy Industry Co. (also known as Hyundae Shipbuilding Company, the largest in the world), Hyundae Automobile Industrial Co., and Hyundae Robot Manufacturing Co. Together, these firms employ almost 70 per cent of the regional manufacturing labour force. The products of Hyundae firms in Ulsan range from paints, metal pipes and elevators to robots, cars and ships. However, they are all in some way or another related to the machine and equipment industry, in which the motor vehicle industry forms the core.

After the 1987 labour dispute, Hyundae Automobile Industrial Co. has undertaken a number of innovative measures; internally, to cope with increasing labour militancy and externally, to build a co-operative network for undisrupted procurement of sophisticated, high quality parts. Computer-controlled equipment, such as numerically controlled lathes, robots, transfer machines and so on, has been introduced on a large scale, and a Just-In-Time (JIT) network has been constructed through the establishment of a multiple-layered hierarchy of subcontracting relationships.

In the middle of the 1970s, major assembly lines in Hyundae Automobile Industrial Co. were largely semi-automatic. Since then, automatic conveyor lines for mass production have been introduced and the new system, reshaped several times in the 1980s, is now fully converted into what Coriat (1991) calls a flexible automation system (or flexible Fordist mass production system). The flexibility of central assembly lines has been enhanced by linking them to other supportive systems such as a Parts Deployment System, a Priority-parts Supply System, a Computer Aided Design System and a Computerized Managerial System. However, contrary to the increased flexibility in the technical arrangement of production, labour processes at shop-floor level remain generally Fordist in the sense that labourers adjust their movements to the speed and flow of conveyer lines, rather than vice versa; which characterizes the classic flexible specialization model.

In particular, workers' autonomous involvement in management is very limited. What is more, these technical innovations have widened the divide between core workers (designers, programmers, technicians, etc.) and peripheral productive workers (simple machinists, service workers, etc.), reflecting the intrinsic trend of large-scale mechanization towards increasing fragmentation of technical processes into de-skilled and re-skilled segments.

On the other hand, the deepening of the division of labour among thousands of units and firms constituting a Just-In-Time network is discernible from the fact that the number of subcontracting firms in automobile industry has increased by approximately 30 per cent from 1985 to 1990. There are now 1940 subcontracting firms.

In the automobile industry, where assembling a car requires more than twenty thousand components, subcontracting between large firms as assemblers and small firms as part suppliers is inevitable. For Hyundae Automobile Industrial Co., as in other Korean motor vehicle manufacturers, subcontracting relations are divided into two broad layers. One is the first layer of subcontracting primarily between large assembly firms and so-called 'Linkage Firms'. These are of two types in turn: either they are reasonably large firms indirectly affiliated to the Group or they are small independent firms with a special co-operative relationship with the group. The first-layer subcontracting firms are for the most of part specialized in producing technical parts such as engine parts, electric/electronic appliances, brake systems, and so on.

The second layer of subcontracting consists mainly in relations between first-layer subcontractors and small firms, most of which carry out narrowly-defined and technically unsophisticated tasks, such as pressing, casting and cutting.

Among the 1940 subcontracting firms in the automobile industry, 540 belong to the first layer of subcontracting and 1400 to the second. In the first layer, mutual technical interdependence based on a functional division of labour is the essential determinant of interfirm relationships. Therefore, quasi-horizontal networking among large and small firms prevails. The second layer is, in contrast, mainly based on relationships which are characteristically vertical and hierarchic. This layer was created when increasing wage costs and labour militancy induced first-layer firms to co-operate with small firms.

Recently, first-layer subcontracting has been intensified, and this has affected the clustering of firms around the focus of lead firms in Ulsan. This phenomenon emerged with the initiation of production innovation in the mid-1980s when standardization and automation of production processes were introduced. Along with technological innovation in lead firms, subcontracting firms were also encouraged not only to comply with new product specifications, but also to keep their production volume in line with the operation of central assembly lines. Further, supplier firms, the technical contribution of which became critical to standardization, and JIT were concentrated in locations close to the lead firms. Presently, about 70 per cent of core first-layer subcontracting firms operate in Ulsan and its surrounding provinces within two hours' reach from the lead firms, although much of the interaction between lead firms and subcontracting firms is carried on through computerized networks in order to synchronize the cross-flows of materials and information.

An important point to be noted here is that spatial concentration happens simultaneously with technological improvement. In other words, the concentration of technical firms around lead firms is a spatial manifestation of the new type of technological and productive interaction. Hence a locality like Ulsan becomes the site of dense networks of technical co-operation between lead firms and subcontracting firms.

However, technological co-operation depends on the technological competence of subcontracting firms. It is therefore not accidental that assisting the technological improvement of subcontracting firms becomes an important part of the productive effort of lead firms. This assistance, encouraged by the new policy for the promotion of the automobile industry, includes technical and financial help, providing high-priced machines, materials and parts, on-site service and manpower training. In the main, this assistance has been successful.

In addition, the improved technological competence of subcontracting firms is expected to lead to the creation of sophisticated niche production, the integration of which in turn leads to the deepening of technological co-operation. Among the most outstanding success of such co-operation is the invention of the 'Alpha engine'. This engine type was the result of a collective technical development project among lead firms and subcontracting firms between 1986 and 1990.

Technological co-operation is also facilitated through varied channels which are not coterminous with technical production networks, such as the Hyundae Co-operation Association, which with Hyundae Motor-vehicle Co. forms with 350 subcontracting firms with strategic roles in the technological division of labour. The Association plays an important role in ensuring the routine and collaborative character of relations between lead firms and followers, within the bounds of contractually defined co-operation. Specification of new products, collective technological development, transfer of technology and machines and the like are dealt with by the Association. It is also important, however, to see that the actual functioning of all these relationships is oiled by inter-personal contacts susceptible to the force of blood ties, school ties and religious affiliation, all being far from pure price mechanisms at work in markets. These human relations are decisively important in businesses based on long-term, stable contracts, financial/technical co-operation, diffusion of key information about new models and smooth settling of bills. In Ulsan this type of relationship forms the organic substratum of interfirm relations.

In summary, the network of automobile production facilitates the functional co-operation of firms with specific technical niches within a geographical system of motor vehicle production. Flexibility of smaller firms facilitates the synchronization of the mass-production processes of lead firms, by establishing quasi-horizontal relationships. These are in turn supported by vertical relations with small firms using elementary techniques. This configuration can be characterized as neo-Fordist.

Textiles and the city of Daegu as a neo-Taylorist area

The textile industry dominated Korea's export-led industrial expansion up to the early 1980s. Hence it is generally agreed that the textile industry was a springboard from which most of the large firms could jump towards technically more demanding and organizationally more complex areas of business. With the decline of the textile business from the early 1980s, large conglomerate firms withdrew their main thrust of business from the textile sector and turned to new high technology projects. Ironically, this change left behind ample room for new high value added textile enterprises.

This new opportunities are most intensely exploited in the city of Daegu in the south-eastern part of Korea. Daegu is the third-largest city in the country and the history of its textile industry goes back to the Japanese colonial period. Currently there are 1966 textile establishments in the Daegu area, accounting for 65.8 per cent of the national total. What is more, 80 per cent of Korea's synthetic textile firms are concentrated in Daegu which is the largest concentration of this activity in the world. Most textile factories are located in government-built industrial estates where every other firm is associated with the textile business.

Production conditions in the textile industry in Daegu are, however, generally backward in character. Not many years ago, the organization of production in textiles used to be extremely notorious for its highly exploitative profile. Long working hours, low wages, patriarchal control and the dominance of cheap female labour characterized this sector. Even now, more than 90 per cent of all textile enterprises employ less than 100 workers and the average rate of obsolescent facilities amounts to 53 per cent.

Because of these repressive labour conditions, the workplaces in Daegu's textile industry were deeply involved in the 1987 nationwide labour unrest. An immediate consequence was a rapid increase of textile workers' wages. In fact, the wages rose by 74 per cent within a year after the dispute, while labour productivity increased by only 21.6 per cent. In addition, new difficulties deriving from the acute shortage of skilled labour afflicted textile firms with a shortage rate of 20 to 25 per cent.

Recognizing the importance of basic consumer industries, the government has brought into effect wide-ranging measures to revitalize the competitiveness of declining industries like textiles and shoes. In the Industrial Development Law enacted in 1986, subsidies were introduced for the installation of new labour-saving high-productivity weaving machines, most of which are equipped with numerical control devices. During 1986–89, 87.4 per cent went to the textile firms in Daegu and its surrounding province, North Kyongsang. Because of this, in 1992, Daegu's share of automated weaving machines in the national stock had gone up to 65 per cent, close to the aggregate level of advanced countries like Italy. But more profound changes which accompany the renovation of production facilities have taken place at the level of intra/interfirm relations.

In response to mounting labour problems such as high wages, labour militancy and labour shortage, and in order to enhance their control possibilities, textile entrepreneurs in Daegu have separated their production processes into several units. Some are particularly capital intensive, others are appropriate for putting-out.

Textile production usually involves four distinct stages: preparation (winding, warping, sizing), dyeing, weaving and packing. The most skill-intensive stage is the third, weaving, stage, where the flexibility of control has improved very much thanks to the above-mentioned high technology machines. Beyond this core activity, flexibility is ensured by the ways in which varied amounts of specific task such as packing and dyeing are put out to small specialized enterprises nearby, whenever needed. Most lead firms maintain open-ended networks for flexible transactions with two to twenty specialized, subcontracting firms.

As a result, in one of the cases studied, the number of full-time wage workers has been reduced from 250 in 1985 to 45 in 1992. Nevertheless, the dominant labour processes on the shop-floor are neo-Taylorist. Although the increased automation of main production lines implies increased technical flexibility, the actual operation of the new facilities does not require sophisticated skills, and even less re-integration of conception and execution.

However, it is certain that production is very adaptable. This stems from the use of flexible techniques as well as transaction networks built among more than 60 small firms or workshops in the area. The number of the firms involved in the network changes from time to time, depending on the type of products, production volumes, labour availability, prices and so on. Of total sales, however, the internally-produced share is less than 30 per cent on average.

What deserves attention is the new division of labour called the 'Little Owner System'. This is a split-up of weaving production lines into several independent units which are run by autonomous managers. The average size of a separate work unit is 50 or 60 looms and owners are usually either former technicians with 20–30 years of experience or former supervisors of production lines. The employees are mainly those who the technicians or the supervisors worked with previously. A workplace has on average less than 20 employees. Initially, production facilities were rented from the parent company, materials were supplied by it, and profit was shared on the basis of a fixed ratio.

Nowadays, new 'little owners' are encouraged to purchase the facilities and run them under their own control. To help in this, not only do parent firms offer financial aid, constant supply contracts and even administrative services, but government-supported organizations like the Small and Medium-Sized Firm Promotion Corporation also operate various aid programmes, including technical services and financial guarantees. The present trend is decreasing size of units, and the core workforce in new enterprises usually consists of the owner and his family. There is a limited number of full-time workers who perform skilled tasks, at times with the help of flexibly employed, that is part-time, assistants. The workplace is usually attached to the residence of the owner. As far as technical matters are concerned, the owners usually possess a broad range of craft-type skills. They know how to set and fix machines, where to buy materials, where to go to find part-time labourers, and where to sell their products.

In this new system, the role of parent firms is also specialized. They keep the technical core part of the production process under their direct control, when some degree of factory automation allows a minimum number of full-time workers. Relieved from the stress deriving from labour control tasks, these firms are instead more and more concerned with improving design quality, getting more production quotas from either other large firms or foreign buyers, and maintaining a coherent transaction network with their associated 'little-owner factories'. Today, due to foreign competition, notably from China, Korean textile manufacturers are compelled to aim at high quality segments of global textile markets.

In consequence, the so-called 'multiple variety, minimum volume' production system has diffused rapidly in the textile industry. One important feature of this system is its dependence on a network where small functional units, each with a special competence, are clustered around parent firms. In Daegu, 86.4 per cent of textile establishments are classified as 'personal workplaces', most of which are 'little owner factories'. These workplaces are located mainly in the periphery of the city and close to large-scale industrial complexes. The ubiquity of this kind of small workshop firms engenders what has been called numerical flexibility, that is, elastic combinations of labourers with new technical skills.

The city of Daegu as a whole is a locality where all elements constituting a system of textile production are tightly knit together. The local wisdom is, that as far as textile industry is concerned, one can find and get whatever needed in Daegu. The textile industry of Daegu extends from threadmaking, through weaving, to clothing. Supportive industries are also thriving. For instance, Daegu's second important industry is metal and machinery, whose historical roots are the manufacture of textile machines and tools. Daegu has also the third-largest traditional market for textiles in Korea.

This relational network permeates the local institutions. For instance, the city government of Daegu is the only one in Korea which has a special administrative department concerned with the textile industry. The same is the case with the Chamber of Trade and Industry. Daegu is the seat of the headquarters of the government-sponsored Textile Research and Promotion Centre which also has located a textile polytechnic there.

Furthermore, all branches of the textile industry in Daegu have their own collaborative associations or co-operatives, such as the Cotton Textile Cooperative, the Silk Producers' Association and the Synthetic Fibre Business Association, to name but a few. In addition, there are many associations of businessmen or workers which represent functionally-defined units, such as the Dyeing Association, the Winders' Association, the Sizing Association, the Packing Association and so on.

In conclusion, the large–small firm network in textiles is geared to combining various types of labour in different work-units. This is achieved by both horizontal quasi-integrative networks as well as numerical flexibility, in terms of labourers employed in individual enterprises and in terms of number of enterprises participating in the network around any given parent company.

Synthesis: towards a theory of flexible specialization

Flexibility as a relational mode

We have shown that as a result of the industrial restructuring under way since the mid-1980s, Korea's overall industrial system has moved one step up in the technological ladder. This restructuring has followed three different technological roads. Along the uppermost road, new hi-tech industries have blossomed. The maturing of traditional capital-intensive industries has followed the middle road. Lastly, the rationalization of traditionally labour-intensive industries has occurred along the lower road.

However, all these levels of industrial change have internalized new productive practices, taking advantage of microelectronics-based technology. Hence, two patterns of industrial change are found on all three levels. One is the internal reorganization of production processes and increasing use of multi-purpose, flexible machines. The other is the externalization of production processes by the construction of complex but flexible interfirm co-operation networks. Seen in this light, flexibility is a key organizational and operational feature of the emerging regime of accumulation (see Martinelli and Schoenberger, 1991).

Flexibility does not flow from the performance of a single unit of production, but from the ways in which all agents, such as a worker with a specific skill, a production line devoted to a particular goods and a factory plant producing a particular commodity, are brought together into a new complex social division of labour (Sayer and Walker, 1992). In the capitalist economy of Korea, large–small firm relations are a key aspect of the new fabric of flexible production relations, in contrast to the conventional model which describes small–small firm networks as the main site of flexibility.

Differences in firm size are closely correlated with differences in technology, manpower composition, organizational capacity, finance, marketing and even access to political power. These differences allow for not only the hierarchical, vertical, obligatory, dependent type of relations, but also the associational, horizontal, interactive, interdependent type in the large–small firm division of labour. The combination of a series of these differentials creates a more dynamic articulation between structure and market, which in turn gives rise to what Coirat (1991) terms 'dynamic flexibility'. In short, the characteristics of the large–small firm relations model allow us to explain not only the global and structural aspect of system performance, but also the local and individual aspect of agent performance. The explanation of the first seems to be generally inadequate in the small–small firm relations model (see Amin and Robin, 1990).

New role of small firms and specialization

Linkages of large and small firms do not come into being anarchically, but are rather consciously built along an extended circuit of commodity production. In weaving the inter-corporate network large firms form central nodes, and a multiplicity of small firms constitute a web around these nodes.

We have claimed that flexibility is derived from the interfirm relations. However, it would be more accurate to say that it is generated by the specialized functions of individual firms/agents working within a system of production. Hence, in order to create a dense interfirm network the role of small firms has to be strengthened *vis à vis* large firms, which are attempting to introduce flexible production into their otherwise Fordist production system.

In Korea, the realization of all these conditions is effectively encouraged by the government, which is at pains to bring about a restructuring of the national economy. With regard to interfirm relations, the main institutional device is the 'Industrial Linkage-Making Promotion Act', the gist of which is to promote, monitor and sanction the co-operation between lead and follower firms involved in inter-linked lines of industrial production.

Yet interfirm relations are also spontaneously fostered beyond such regulatory schemes. The social production of new products such as hi-tech consumer durables requires large and small firms alike to seek mutual assistance and co-operation in practice. Of interest is that this interchange takes place for the most part in the way that large firms help small weak firms by means of providing high-priced machines and finance technical assistance, on-site service, requisite materials and parts, market outlets, and so on. Recently this trend has been intensified in conjunction with the introduction of varied 'Schemes for the Transfer or Large Firm's Business to Small Firms'. The transfer comprises not only hardware items like machines/facilities, but also software items like patents, organizational know-how and manpower, both accompanied by financial aid and institutional guarantees from either large private firms or quasi-government organizations like the Small and Medium Industry Promotion Corporation. In many cases the actual transaction is mediated by personal relationships though nominally subject to associations' codes and legal guidelines.

Large firms' assistance to small firms, however, must be appreciated from the view of it being essentially geared to the need for promoting specialization of the latter. For large firms, the specialization of small firms creates something outside the parent firm which either is absent or highly costly to retain in-house. On the other hand, for small firms, specialization creates opportunities for technical improvement, managerial stability, better profit and so on. Thus, the social process of specialization inherently presupposes a division of labour and intensified relations among large and small enterprises.

This type of arrangement is advantageous both to lead firms who lack sufficient capacity, expertise or power to lower wage costs, and follower firms who lack adequate market outlets, financing and technical or managerial skills. In a specialized division of labour, the interaction between large and small firms facilitates the exchange of ideas, materials and manpower to solve specific problems of design, manufacture and marketing under specific production and labour-service contracts. The catalyst of such outcome is the collective efficiency which the networking of large and small firms based on specialization creates in the course of its operation (Schmitz, 1989).

Space, clustering and a flexible regime of accumulation

The networking leading to specialization tends to be furthered with interaction in a local context. Geographical nearness allows for easier knowledge-sharing and exchange of ideas, materials and labour, as well as benefiting from local supportive services. When such geographical conditions are bound up with those of productive organization, they work as a stimulus to the furtherance of specialization which would not exist if geographically remote or separated. From this viewpoint, we can define the concentration of inter-related activities in a locality as a geographically facilited form of specialization, constituted by dense interfirm networking along a productive circuit within a particular local setting. In our study, this refers to the geographical clustering of inter-related small firms around the foci of large firms.

The ways in which large and small firms are clustered differ from one locality to another. An individual cluster comprises an idiosyncratic constellation of interfirm relations, such as technical co-operation, production linkages, service and financial ties, marketing arrangements, business associations, local infrastructures and local labour markets. It has been shown that in line with the three levels of technological change, three regional clusters have been emerging. Taken together, the three archetypal techno-spatial clusters combine to mould the complex of Korea's new industrial system that takes shape in conjunction with recent industrial restructuring. Each cluster has its own pattern of interfirm relations and resultant flexibility.

Our final remark is that there is no single pathway to a flexible specialization industrialization paradigm. In particular, the 'new orthodoxy' based on Piore and Sabel's paradigmatic theorization of flexibility drawing upon a single type of small–small firm relations leaves many important questions unasked and unanswered.

MEXICAN MANUFACTURERS

9 Industrial districts in Mexico: The case of the footwear industry in Guadalajara and Leon

ROBERTA RABELLOTTI

In this paper we will present some results of a wider research project aimed at elaborating an international comparative study among industrial districts in Italy and in developing countries. Particularly, we have carried out an investigation of the footwear industry in two areas of specialization in Italy and two in Mexico.[1] Only the results of the Mexican case study will be presented here.

The general objective of the study is to analyse some clusters of small enterprises, namely geographical and sectoral concentration of firms, putting on 'industrial district spectacles'. The question is whether these agglomerations can simply be represented as the sum of their components or if they can better be identified as *holistic systems*, namely systems characterized by a higher degree of efficiency than the pure sum of efficiencies of their single agents.

We define an industrial district as a dynamic network of agents interacting in a specific economic area under particular, although sometimes implicit, institutional and behavioural rules, involved in the production and marketing of a particular product. The interactions among agents are flows of goods as well as flows of knowledge, information and people and therefore they go far beyond the simple exchange of inputs and outputs through the market.

Our aim is to understand in a detailed way the mechanisms of generation of synergies among the components of the district and therefore to explain the phenomenon called 'collective efficiency' by some scholars (Schmitz, 1990; 1992) and external economies by others (Becattini, 1989; 1990).

However, in this paper we do not want to enter into the theoretical debate on what exactly is the definition of concepts such as 'collective efficiency' or external economies. For the moment we rather hope to be able to contribute to better understanding of these very complex and tricky concepts, reporting some empirical results of the different aspects they include.

We will therefore present the results of research which has been carried out in two clusters of footwear enterprises, Guadalajara and Leon, in Mexico. Both areas have the critical mass needed to be studied in an 'industrial district' perspective: Leon and Guadalajara have respectively 1700 and 1200-odd enterprises of a total of 4500 firms in the whole of Mexico.[2] Moreover, in both towns there are backward and forward-linked firms and institutions devoted to the assistance of the footwear sector.

The research has consisted in interviewing a sample of 51 footwear enterprises with a rather structured questionnaire,[3] aimed at obtaining information about performance, linkages with suppliers and market, strategies of process and product innovation, organization of production process, linkages with public and private institutions and finally strategies of investments.

To complement the information obtained from the analysis of the questionnaires, apart from the available official sources, a number of open interviews have been undertaken with key informers such as suppliers, traders, institutions and sector experts.

The paper is structured as follows: in the next section the main characteristics of the footwear industry in Mexico will be briefly presented, in the following one the results of our case studies will be synthesized and finally some conclusions will be put forward in the last section.

The Mexican footwear industry

Recent performance

Mexico has been for long time a protected market, having adopted an import-substitution strategy, which was drastically abandoned in 1988 with the opening up of the economy to foreign competition. The Mexican footwear industry therefore, being protected from international competition, has for many decades produced mainly for the domestic market with a rate of growth strictly linked with the increase in the domestic demand (Table 9.1). The level of domestic per capita consumption of shoes, which sustained the growth of the industry, has traditionally been higher in Mexico than in other developing countries. In 1985–87 the average per capita consumption rate in developing countries was 0.3 pairs per year, while in Mexico it was three pairs (ILO, 1992). However, notwithstanding its high relative level, in 1991 per capita consumption decreased to 2.4 pairs per year as a consequence of the decline in real wages (Dominguez-Villalobos and Brown-Grossman, 1992).

Together with the fall of domestic demand, the acceleration of the opening up of the Mexican market to international competition, through the elimination of import licensing and tariff reduction[4] had a very heavy impact on the footwear industry. The market was flooded with imports which increased from 2.2 millions of pairs in 1987 to 38.2 in 1991 (SECOFI, 1992).

Although the Mexican footwear industry is threatened by the increasing international competition, on the other hand it has a unique opportunity to massively enter in the US market.[5] Mexico has signed a Free Trade Agreement with the US and Canada and the Mexican shoe producers will be able to take advantage of the elimination of duties and of the proximity to the US market. Mexico could possibly become in a few years one of the world's leading exporters of footwear.

Table 9.1 Trends in output and employment in the Mexican footwear and leather industry

Year	Overall GDP (m.pesos 1980=100)	Leather and footwear GDP (m.pesos 1980=100)	Number workers (leather and footwear)	Exports US$m.	Imports US$m.
1970	2 359 000	16 095.47	97 555	3.40	15.50
1975	3 238 800	21 809.06	118 292	12.10	28.80
1978	3 780 500	25 545.50	121 670	25.20	19.00
1979	4 126 600	28 935.28	138 155	30.80	17.10
1980	4 470 100	29 666.00	138 909	32.00	62.00
1981	4 862 200	32 652.00	152 303	24.40	67.30
1982	4 831 700	32 609.00	155 706	21.70	13.10
1983	4 628 900	27 792.00	130 521	15.30	4.60
1984	4 796 000	29 370.00	131 478	29.00	11.90
1985	4 920 400	30 284.00	135 390	24.40	15.70
1986	4 732 100	28 623.00	135 666	31.00	9.40
1987	4 802 400	24 686.00	128 875	86.10	13.70
1988	4 855 200	24 071.00	119 578	118.00	54.30
1989	5 024 226	24 902.00	117 529	117.20	112.80
Growth rates (per cent)					
1970–78	6.10	5.25	2.48	24.93	2.29
1978–81	8.74	6.33	5.77	–0.80	37.19
1982–89	0.60	–3.78	–3.94	27.24	36.01

Source: Dominguez-Villalobos, 1992.

The challenge the Mexican footwear industry is facing in these days is therefore rather extreme. The alternatives are a progressive reduction in the number of firms, because of the increasing competition in the domestic market of imported shoes from countries like Taiwan, China and Korea, or the acquisition of a leading position as an exporter in the international market.

For many decades the domestic producers took advantage from a market where demand was greater than supply; to make money in the sector was relatively easy because every kind of product was sold, no matter its quality, design and cost. Nowadays, international competition is becoming stronger and stronger and the Mexican footwear enterprises are starting to realize they have to increase their efficiency if they want to survive and grow. Many firms are currently looking for a revitalization strategy to adopt, in order to increase their competitiveness in the international and domestic markets.

The industrial district way of organizing production, which has been so successful in the case of the Italian footwear industry, is actually one of the models the Mexican shoe entrepreneurs are now analysing with greater attention, considering the potentialities for its applicability to the Mexican reality.

The structure of the sector

The artisanal origin of the Mexican footwear industry explains the bias towards small size of its firms; in fact, according to the last available industrial census (1980) 86.5 per cent of firms employ less than 50 employees (30 per cent of total employment) and produce 23 per cent of total value added, 12 per cent employ between 50 and 250 employees (37 per cent of total employment) producing 37 per cent of total value added and only 1.5 per cent employ more than 250 employees (33 per cent of total employment) producing 40 per cent of total value added.

From the spatial point of view the sector is highly concentrated in three different areas: 37 per cent of the officially registered 4500 firms is located in Leon, 27 per cent in Mexico City and its outskirts (Districto Federal), 26 per cent in Guadalajara while the remaining 10 per cent is spread out in the rest of the country (CICEG, 1990).

Besides, the three main areas of production are strongly specialized: Leon mainly produces men's and children's shoes, Guadalajara, women's shoes and the Districto Federal, athletic shoes.

Considering the division of total production in the different segments of market, 12 per cent is in the high quality segment, 50 per cent in the medium one and 38 per cent in the economic segment (CANAICAL, 1991).

It is important to emphasize that the sector is almost completely owned by Mexican capital, only four enterprises in the country have a foreign majority share holding. In the footwear industry the phenomenon of *maquilladoras*[6] is more limited than in other sectors, like for instance electronics, cars and clothing; in 1990 the number of employees in the leather and footwear *maquilladora* industry was about 7000, which is 5 per cent of total employment in the sector.

Finally, as we have said, the vast majority of firms were born as artisanal and many of them are still owned by the same family.

In summary, the sector is dominated by small and medium-sized family firms, spatially concentrated in three different, highly specialized areas. These are the first, basic characteristics of the industrial district model; the existence of such an agglomeration of firms at least should justify the attempt to look at this reality with a 'systemic' approach.

The results of the case studies

The sample

We have interviewed in 51 enterprises: 30 of them are located in Guadalajara and 21 in Leon. We have chosen our sample in order to include firms of different size: 17 enterprises employ less than 50 employees, 14 between 51 and 99 employees and 20 more than 100 employees. In the two clusters the sample is as following: in Guadalajara 12 firms are small, 9 are medium and 9 are large and in Leon 5 are small, 5 medium and 11 large. This composition takes into account the real structure of the footwear industry in the two areas with regard to size; in Leon most of the large enterprises in the country are concentrated and in fact the size structure is: 45 per cent small enterprises, 45 per cent medium ones and 10 per cent large (CICEG, 1990). In Guadalajara there is a stronger concentration of small firms: they are about 80 per cent while the remaining 20 per cent are medium and large firms, according to estimates of the local *Camara*.

With regard to product specialization, 42 firms produce women's shoes, 12 make men's shoes and 17 produce children's shoes. Not every firm is specialized in just one type of shoe, as 14 of them produce a mix of products.

Taking in consideration the age of the firms, ten of them have been established since before 1959, six from 1960 to 1969, 13 from 1970 to 1979 and 22 after 1980. Almost 70 per cent of the firms have therefore been established after 1970; however, it is important to emphasize that some of the new firms are in fact old firms transformed into new companies for fiscal reasons and others have been recently created by second-generation entrepreneurs, who decided to diversify the activity of their family, entering into a new segment of market.

There are also a few cases of firms established by people who have been working for a long time in other firms of the area, frequently as supervisors. Very often they have been helped by their old employers to start up a new firm and then they mainly work as subcontractors for them.

From the point of view of its origin our sample is therefore very much in line with the 'industrial district' model, according to which most of the firms starts up as a family business and from which other firms are generated as a spin-off effect.

The performance

Unfortunately, sale value can not be taken as a good indicator of performance because of the high inflation rate of the Mexican economy during the last years.[7]

A more interesting indicator of performance is the trend of net profits. During the last five years the profits of 35 per cent of the firms have increased, 27 per cent have remained stable and another 27 per cent have decreased. The trend of net profits is positively correlated with the trend of employment: 40 per cent of the firms which have increased employment have also obtained an increase in profits, 50 per cent of the firms with stable employment have registered stable profits and finally, 71 per cent of the firms with decreasing employment have suffered a decrease in their profits.

The sample firms have also been asked to evaluate their profits in 1990: 20 per cent declared a good profit, 45 per cent a regular profit, 12 per cent no profit at all and another 12 per cent a loss.

Considering the relationships between net profit and size, small enterprises earn less profit than medium and large ones: 53 per cent of the small firms have not obtained any profit (29 per cent) or have suffered a loss (24 per cent), while this was the case for only 21 per cent of the medium and 15 per cent of the large firms. Of the large firms, 65 per cent have earned a regular profit and 15 per cent of them a good profit; for the medium firms the results are 36 per cent and 29 per cent; and for the small firms 29 per cent and 18 per cent.

Another indicator of performance we have taken into account is the number of pairs of shoes produced per year: in 1990 29 per cent of the firms have produced less than 50,000 pairs, 16 per cent between 50,000 and 100,000, 24 per cent between 100,000 and 200,000, 18 per cent between 200,000 and 500,000 and finally, 13 per cent more than 500,000. During the last five years, 67 per cent of the firms have increased the number of produced pairs, 13 per cent have kept their level of production while another 13 per cent have decreased their production volume.

Finally, taking into consideration the trend of employment during the last five years, in 70 per cent of the firms employment has increased, while in 15 per cent it has remained stable and in 14 per cent it has decreased. There are not important differences of behaviour between firms located in Leon and Guadalajara nor between firms of different size.

The labour market

Analysing the characteristics of the labour market, the main problems emphasized by the sample firms are: the low availability of qualified workforce (73 per cent of the firms), the high turnover of the labour force (28 per cent), the low availability of unqualified workforce (24 per cent) and finally absenteeism (20 per cent).

Skilled labour is a scarce resource and therefore qualified workers require relatively high salaries and favourable conditions of work; this explains why 82 per cent of small and 71 per cent of medium firms, which usually pay lower salaries and offer more unstable conditions of work, due to irregularities of orders, find it difficult to hire them.

With regard to unskilled labour, this represents a less important problem because there exists a large reservoir of young people, mainly women, available to work. The main problem with unskilled labour is turnover, because workers move out from the footwear sector as soon as they find a job in other, more remunerative, sectors or, in the case of women, when they get married.

Competition from other sectors to recruit people is higher in Guadalajara than in Leon, where the footwear and leather sectors are the main manufacturing activities. However, in the near future, even in Leon this could become a major problem, according to many entrepreneurs, who are afraid the Free Trade Agreement will attract a lot of foreign investment in sectors other than the traditional footwear and leather industries. The attractiveness of the region in which Leon is located is explained by its strategical geographical position, just north of Mexico City, along the highway to the United States. The eventual establishment in the area of other more remunerative sectors will oblige Leon's shoe entrepreneurs to look for alternative locations for their firms outside the town, in the countryside, where there is still a great availability of unskilled, cheap labour. The local *Camara* is already moving in that direction and a few enterprises have started an experiment of decentralization of some phases of production outside Leon, to overcome the rising difficulties on the labour market.

The need to increase salaries, in order to be attractive for the workforce, could become a problem if it reduces the competitiveness of labour costs with respect to other international competitors. Nowadays the Mexican cost of labour in the sector is in fact in line with countries like Brazil, Korea or Taiwan and there is not much space left for further increases, unless productivity increases.

Another aspect related to labour force we have investigated in our survey is training. In most of the sample firms (48 per cent) training takes place inside the same firms. In 45 per cent of the firms, some training is also obtained from external institutions like the local *Camara*.

This happens more frequently in large (50 per cent) and medium (29 per cent) firms, mainly located in Guadalajara (62 per cent). External training is generally reserved for supervisors, technicians or designers; less skilled workers like edgers are very rarely trained outside the firms.

A problem emphasized by many interviewed firms is the risk of losing workers sent to be trained outside, because they find a better paid job. This is a very common problem among small-scale enterprises, which usually pay lower salaries than larger firms: a typical case of market failure which justifies some kind of extra-market intervention to make up for resistance of firms to training their workforce externally.

Technological and organizational changes

During the eighties a process of decapitalization took place in the footwear industry with a consequent diffused obsolescence of the existing equipment. Data on investments in the textile, clothing, leather and footwear industry confirm this trend: from 1981 to 1987 expenditures in machines and technical equipment decreased from 1249 million pesos to 234 million at constant prices.

The process of decapitalization is also confirmed by a recent study carried out by Dominguez-Villalobos and Brown-Grossman (1992), according to which most of the 18 interviewed firms declared that in the last five years they did not acquire any new machines.

However, according to a study carried out by Boston Consulting Group (1988) the obsolescence of equipment is not one of the major problems in the Mexican footwear industry, but rather the lack of specialized machines as a constraint for improving productivity in specific phases.

In our own enquiry we have asked the interviewed firms to evaluate their own tendency to innovate in the last five years: 14 per cent of them have declared to have not introduced any technological innovations, 33 per cent to have introduced very small innovations, 35 per cent some innovations and finally 18 per cent important innovations (12 per cent of them have declared they have been the first in their area).

As it could be expected the most innovative firms are the large ones (35 per cent have introduced important innovations and 40 per cent some innovations), while 82 per cent of the small firms have introduced very small innovations or do not innovate at all.

The relationship between innovation and profit is rather favourable for innovative firms: 20 per cent of the firms which have obtained a very good profit have also introduced important innovations, 50 per cent some innovations, 20 per cent small innovations and 10 per cent no innovations at all; for the firms which have obtained a regular profit the percentages are respectively: 17 per cent, 39 per cent, 35 per cent and 9 per cent. Taking into account the trend of profits, 78 per cent of the highly innovative firms have registered an increasing (56 per cent) or stable (22 per cent) profit and for the regularly innovative ones the percentages are 35 per cent and 41 per cent; while 33 per cent of the low innovative firms and 50 per cent of the firms which do not innovate have registered a decreasing profit. On the grounds of these figures we can therefore conclude that innovation can favourably influence performance, but apparently it is not the only aspect on which the interviewed enterprises have based their strategy of growth and in fact the lack of process innovation does not necessarily hamper a positive result in our sample.

A very interesting result coming out from our inquiry and also from the other recent studies we have quoted before (Dominguez-Villalobos and Brown-Grossman, 1992; and Boston Consulting Group, 1988) is the rather diffused tendency among the most innovative firms to introduce, besides technological innovations, organizational innovations.

The model for reorganizing the production process for most of the firms is the pair-by-pair methodology widely adopted in the Brazilian footwear industry, based on the idea that the cycle of production is a continuum and it has to be completed as soon as a pair enters the assembly line, while in the traditional way of organizing production every single phase is considered as a separate entity from the other ones.

In terms of organizational techniques, this innovative way of production implies work group technology, replacing conveyor belts, and moreover a new payment system, substituting a piece-rate system with a system based on the production of the whole cell. The expected advantages are: first, a reduction of inventories; second, an increase in labour flexibility; third, a greater uniformity in quality; and finally a cut down of 'dead' time (Prochnik, 1992).

With the adoption of these new organizational models firms seem to have room for increase in productivity even in the absence of new costly investments in technology. Besides, it is well known that if technological innovations are not complemented with changes in the organizational system, the effect on firms' efficiency can be very limited or, sometimes, even negative. This strategy seems therefore a very promising one but, unfortunately, at the moment we can not go very far from these speculations because these organizational changes are too recent for us to be able to evaluate their real impact on firms' performance.

The suppliers

According to several recent surveys (Boston Consulting Group, 1988; Dominguez-Villalobos and Brown-Grossman, 1992) the Mexican footwear industry is highly vertically integrated for two main reasons: first of all backward-linked industries have reached a very low degree of development with regard to quality, design and service; secondly, in the sector there is a lack of a standard technical language and of a common, universally accepted measurement system.

Therefore, the poor level of development and the difficulties of communication with the backward linked industries have induced many shoe firms to internalize as many phases of the production cycle as possible, in order to reduce their dependency on an unstable, low quality supply. However, this strategy has often generated negative results with regard to economic efficiency and specialization because the different phases of the footwear production cycle are characterized by different economies of scale and require different skills.

According to the quoted study by Boston Consulting Group, in Mexico 95 per cent of leather soles for children's shoes, 90 per cent for men's and 65 per cent for women's are produced inside the shoe enterprises; while, for instance, in Italy 80 per cent of leather components is produced in specialized, independent firms.

The low tendency to decentralize some phases of production outside the firms is confirmed by the results of our investigation: although 76 per cent of the sample firms have decentralized some processes, only 20 per cent of the firms have in fact decentralized more than 50 per cent of edging and sewing, 33 per cent decentralized completely the production of soles and insoles and, finally, 27 per cent decentralized a particular kind of puckered seam, highly labour intensive, which characterizes moccasins.

The firms decentralizing some phases of production are slightly more concentrated in Leon (86 per cent) than in Guadalajara (70 per cent) and this is confirmed by the higher tendency of large firms (41 per cent) to decentralize than of medium (26 per cent) and small ones (33 per cent).

A very interesting result is the positive relation between decentralization and performance: 47 per cent of the firms which decentralize have obtained a regular profit, 21 per cent a very good profit, while only 10 per cent made no profit at all and 13 per cent a loss (for firms which do not decentralize the percentages are respectively: 33, 16, 16 and 33 per cent). With regard to the trend of profits the results are very similar: in the last five years 37 per cent of the decentralizing firms have obtained an increase in their profits (for firms which do not decentralize the percentages are: 33, 17 and again 33 per cent).

Decentralization, even if it is a rather limited phenomenon, seems therefore to have a positive effect on performance and from that we could conclude firms should be encouraged to decentralize more. However, a system of production based on a strong division of labour, such as for instance the Italian one, necessarily requires a very well developed network of suppliers, and this is definitely not the case in Mexico.

The sample firms generally complain about the low quality of components, the scarce attention for fashion changes and the bad service their suppliers very often provide. It appears that in Guadalajara firms meet with more difficulties with suppliers than in Leon, where most of the backward-linked enterprises are located.

Naturally suppliers do not accept the complete responsibility for their limited development; in fact they accuse shoe entrepreneurs of having always adopted a strategy more focused on price than quality. Suppliers therefore complain about a very unstable demand of very small batches of orders of continuously-changing products, and about the delays in payments.

We seem to have a two-sided problem where both the suppliers of components and the manufacturers blame each other and the main problem is probably communication and collaboration among the two linked sectors. Only strong collaboration among them will make possible to produce an internationally competitive product.

Recently, the importance of a systemic view of the production process is emerging. For instance, in Leon the associations of suppliers and footwear firms are starting to work together on fashion content and standardization of measurement systems. There are also cases of continuous and productive collaboration among some shoe firms and for instance some tanneries: a stable demand allows a stable level of quality of the supplied leather. Some distribution companies are also working in that direction, organizing the purchases of components of all their clients and therefore guaranteeing large and stable orders to the suppliers. In both Guadalajara and Leon the local Credit Unions of shoe entrepreneurs have also launched a programme for common purchasing.

These are a few examples of initiatives trying to foster the systemic approach, showing a real effort towards building up a system of production in some way inspired by the 'industrial district' model. In our case studies we have found a relatively high intensity of backward linkages within the districts; however in many cases, these linkages need re-qualification because they are based only on a price factor, disregarding important aspects like fashion, quality of materials, delivery time, design. In this regard an intensive policy at association level is needed to make entrepreneurs understand the issue and to launch and co-ordinate initiatives of collaboration among suppliers of components and raw materials and manufacturers.

Distribution and market

The interviewed firms produce for different segments of the market: 22 per cent of them are specialized in the high segment, 53 per cent in the medium one, 16 per cent in the economic one, while the remaining 9 per cent produce for a mix of segments.

It is interesting that firms in the upper market tend to be very innovative. In fact 27 per cent of them have introduced important innovations, 45 per cent have been moderately innovative and finally 30 per cent have introduced small innovations. On the other hand, 62 per cent of the firms producing for the economic segment of the market have introduced only very small innovations.

With regard to distribution channels, in 73 per cent of the firms' products are sold by non-exclusive agents, in 51 per cent by wholesalers and finally in 16 per cent by distribution companies or shops owned by the firms. Most of the firms therefore sell their products by means of more than one channel, only 27 per cent of them use exclusively agents, and 10 per cent wholesalers.

General information on the structure of distribution are scarce and mainly based on estimates reported in the study of Boston Consulting Group (1988). According to these estimates, in 1987 independent retailers had around 41 per cent of the market, chains had 20 per cent, supermarkets had 19 per cent and the remaining 20 per cent was distributed by wholesalers.

One of the main consequences of a distribution system dominated by independent retailers is the small size of orders: according to the Boston Consulting Group study the most common size of orders in the domestic market is around 300 pairs. The limited size of orders is a positive feature in the high segment of market, where one of the competitive advantages of firms is the ability to produce many different models, in line with the last fashion indications.

However, the size of orders by chains, supermarkets and foreign buyers is definitely larger, around 4000 pairs per model, and it can reach even 10,000 pairs in the case of the export market. The inability of the Mexican footwear enterprises to satisfy large orders becomes therefore a limitation above all in the export market. It is rather common that Mexican firms have to refuse orders from US buyers because they are unable to satisfy large orders.

In 1991 only 6 per cent of overall production was exported: 16 millions of pairs of a total value of US$ 81 million (SECOFI, 1992) mainly athletic shoes produced in the *maquilladora* industry, located along the border with USA and *botas vaqueros* (cowboy boots), a segment of market in which the Mexican footwear industry has traditionally been very competitive. More recently, exports of men's shoes of medium and high quality have increased significantly (CANAICAL, 1991).

The export market is dominated by foreign buyers who impose their models on Mexican firms and choose their suppliers according to quality and price of their products. Mexican firms are therefore completely dependent on the buyers and do not have direct access and knowledge of the US market. A very evident sign of this dependence is the unstable performance of exports declared by many among the interviewed firms.

In our sample, 33 per cent of the firms' exports, 10 per cent of them were less than 10 per cent of their sale volume, 15 per cent between 10 per cent and 40 per cent, and finally 8 per cent more than 40 per cent. The more export-oriented firms are large enterprises, located in Leon, where firms producing boots and men's shoes, which we have seen are the most exported types of shoes, are concentrated.

In the case of domestic retail chains the footwear firms also very often have a position of dependency. These chains generally adopt a strategy based on the search for the lowest possible price on the market. Many stories are told about some of these chains contacting some firms to copy their models and then contracting other firms, in the illegal market, to produce the same products at a lower price.

Recently, a few wholesalers have started to adopt a new kind of strategy, aimed at selling a quality product and have therefore selected a group of shoe firms with which to develop a stable and constructive relationship. Technician employees of the wholesalers visit the shoe enterprises regularly, controlling quality and giving free consultancies on technological and organizational matters; moreover the wholesalers organize a system of common purchases of some key components or raw materials like leather in order to guarantee a stable level of quality, better prices and good service. Among our interviewed firms, the ones linked by such a relationship with wholesalers are generally very satisfied, not only for the realized sales, but above all for the complementary services they receive; many of them have been able to introduce important improvements in the organization of production processes and in the quality of their products, thanks to the collaboration with these wholesalers.

Commercialization is one of the weakest points of the Mexican footwear industry because of fragmentation of distribution channels, dependency of producers on agents, chains or foreign buyers and very low direct knowledge of the market. The Mexican enterprises have not traditionally cared a lot about commercialization because, due to the protection of the domestic market, competition has for a long time been very low.

However, after the opening up of the domestic market in the sector there is a general agreement that commercialization aspects deserve more attention, but these are very complex and expensive investments for small firms to carry on by themselves. A search for a new strategy, likely based on co-operation among firms in order to increase their bargaining power and to improve their access to information and knowledge of the market, is therefore one of the most important issues the Mexican shoe enterprises will have to tackle in the near future.

Formal and informal co-operation among firms

In our sample several enterprises (39 per cent) own equity shares of other firms and, rather obviously, these are mainly large firms (75 per cent). Backward and forward integration seem therefore to be the most common strategy of growth among our sample firms and, particularly, there are ten cases of integration towards the component industry and fifteen cases towards the market. Besides, there are seven cases of horizontal integration with other shoe firms and four cases of participation in sectors not related with the footwear industry.

In the case of backward integration the main objective, as we have already seen, is to avoid the dependency on a low quality and unstable supply of components and raw materials; however, the risk is to enter a different sector without the required know-how and consequently a lack of specialization. Forward integration is instead aimed at first appropriating the large margin of profit of commercialization. Second, it has a positive effect in terms of image and market success of a brand name and third, it reduces dependency on market agents, increasing market control and access to information.

The relation between performance and participation in other firms is positive: 80 per cent of the firms with some kind of participation has obtained a good (50 per cent) or a very good (30 per cent) profit. Furthermore in the last five years, in 35 per cent of them profits have increased and in 25 per cent have remained stable.

In 33 per cent of the firms there are also some cases of non-equity agreements: twelve firms have established technological agreements, nine subcontracting agreements and six commercial agreements. Technological and commercial co-operation is very often among firms linked by family ties exchanging technological information on a regular basis and, when needed, machines, and moreover selling their products jointly. Some cases of technological co-operation are also among firms and distribution companies which, as we have seen in the previous section, supply technological consultancy and work together with firms to adapt technology and organize efficiently the production process.

According to the interviewed firms, the main reasons for co-operation are the access to new markets (ten firms), the increase in availability of information (nine firms) and finally the reduction of costs (six firms).

Informal co-operation is very frequent in 80 per cent of the sample firms and it is considered an important asset by almost all of them (96 per cent). The role of the entrepreneurial associations seems to be very important in inducing informal co-operation among firms because, according to 37 firms, events organized by the *Camara* are the most important occasions of informal exchanges with their colleagues. Family ties have also an important role in 17 firms and, finally, social events are important for 11 firms.

The informal co-operation intervenes in many different aspects of firm life, among which there are exchanges of technological and market information, exchanges of machines and workers, sub-contracting of orders in case of excess demand, joint commercialization, joint purchases of inputs, joint recovery of credits.

A very interesting result that it is important to emphasize is the preference of 65 per cent of the interviewed firms for more formal agreements, in the sense of more stable and organized relationships and other firms. The *agrupamientos industriales* promoted by the *Camara del Calzado* in Guadalajara are an attempt in that direction. The initiative started seven years ago, based on a methodology proposed by the World Bank, in the shape of a course for managers: the participants had to agree to open their own enterprises to the other entrepreneurs taking part in the group and to allow an external expert (business students in their last year) to make a diagnosis of their firms. In seven years, seven groups, involving about 120 enterprises, have been started in this way and afterwards they have carried on meeting regularly to discuss problems related to technology, marketing, suppliers, etc. and to exchange information about clients, machines, workers, orders. The role of the *Camara* has been crucial in such initiatives because it has designed the initial framework of collaboration and above all it has promoted the idea and induced the 'need for co-operation' among entrepreneurs.

Institutional support

A number of important institutions have been identified both in Guadalajara and in Leon, some being associations of firms, others providing special services to the industries involved in the footwear *filière*.

The associations of entrepreneurs (*Camara del Calzado*) are the most important institutions supporting the footwear industry in Mexico; there are three local associations, in Guadalajara, Leon and Mexico City, and a national one with the aim of co-ordinating the activities of the three local ones.

The role of these associations is to supply services like fiscal and labour consultancy, commercial assistance, managerial training, organization of trade fairs and to lobby at political level.

Every firm in our sample is associated to the local *Camara de Calzado* and in general we have found a more positive assessment of the supplied services in Guadalajara than in Leon.

Both in Guadalajara and in Leon there is also a Credit Union aimed at obtaining credit for its members at more favourable conditions than market ones. In Guadalajara the Credit Union, which has been created as an initiative of an *agrupamiento industrial*, also manages a programme for joint purchases.

Moreover, in Guadalajara there is the *Instituto Tecnologico del Calzado*, linked with the *Camara*, which is devoted to training and technological research. It is a relatively new initiative, established in 1984, which has set up a diversified programme for training addressed to designers, manual skilled workers like edgers but also managers and entrepreneurs.

Finally, in Leon there exists a centre for technological support called CIATEG, created with the objective to supply technical and quality control services to the footwear industry at national level; in fact it is mainly used by Leon's enterprises, leaving shoe firms in the rest of Mexico almost without any technological support.

The existence of a relatively well-developed institutional network of support to the footwear *filière* is a very important condition in the case of adoption of a growth strategy based on a systemic approach. Institutions like the *Camara del Calzado* can have a very relevant role in diffusing among entrepreneurs a systemic vision of their business, in other words the idea that the survival and growth of their own firms strongly depends on the development of the whole system of shoe firms, suppliers, buyers, market agents, service firms and supporting institutions.

We have seen that among the components of the analysed cluster of firms some forms of explicit co-operation and many cases of unconscious collaboration already exist; however, to really implement an 'industrial district' model of development, or in other words to better exploit collective efficiency or/and external economies, the role of institutions is unavoidable.

Some tentative conclusions

As we stated at the beginning of the paper, our aim in the analysis of the results of our case studies was to understand if the two considered clusters of enterprises could be represented as the mere sum of the economic agents located there or, instead, something more could be found. Our results have shown quite clearly that interactions among agents within the clusters are rather intense and do not consist only of flows of goods but flows of information, knowledge and people are also rather significant.

We have asked our sample firms to identify their main factors of strength and these were reported to be quality of products (according to 49 per cent of the firms), skill of labour force (31 per cent), availability of information (18 per cent) and institutional support (18 per cent). Therefore, three out of four main factors can in some way be related with clustering of firms.

However, firms have also been asked to identify their main factors of weakness and they are: low availability of labour (according to 39 per cent of the firms), lack of a commercial strategy (35 per cent) and finally, low availability of components and services (31 per cent). In this case therefore two of three main weaknesses show a limited development of some of the positive effects clustering should offer.

In a dynamic framework of analysis, we would like to distinguish between industrial district Mark I and Mark II (Brusco, 1990): the first model is characterized by spontaneous, bottom-up development and the second one by explicit intervention which either did not exist before, or was at least less evident.

In our case studies spontaneous development has reached a certain stage which we have tried to explain in detail in this paper; naturally the story of these development processes is unique because they are characterized by a unique set of initial and external conditions. However, it seems rather evident from our results that 'collective efficiency' or/and external economies have a positive impact on growth, although they are still rather underdeveloped in the analysed systems of firms. It seems therefore reasonable to suggest that it could be opportune to take a step forward and start the Mark II stage.

On how to bring about collective efficiency and/or external economies, the results of our next step of research, a comparative analysis with footwear industrial districts in Italy, could probably be very useful.

10 Reflections on the present predicament of the Mexican garment industry

FIONA WILSON

In this paper I want to argue for the importance of taking a more reflexive approach to industrialization processes. It appears increasingly necessary for researchers to encompass both what is going on, on the ground as it were, in specific industrial sectors or clusters, and what are the major tendencies in the air, that are moulding the wider political economy and thus the opportunities and limitations confronting industrial activity. One needs to experiment more often by taking different viewpoints, moving scales, and shifting levels of abstraction so as to alternate between one approach and another. Adopting a double macro–micro vision at one and the same time is not always appropriate or possible within the framework of a single enquiry, nor are researchers necessarily in a position to observe or delineate linkages between the two arenas of analysis until detailed work has been done on each.

The aim of this paper is to move away from a locality-based case study in Mexico, and to begin to take stock of the magnitude of the economic and political transformations affecting that country during the 1980s and enquire into the ways that trade liberalization and economic restructuring are affecting small-scale garment production.

I shall start by elaborating on the importance of reflexivity by referring to my previous work. This study explored some of the industrial processes underway in a broad region of central western Mexico. Here, I shall take up some points coming through from fieldwork in a single small town as to the experience of expansion and contraction in a branch of the garment sector, sweater production. Then I shall move focus to examine the main characteristics of the garment-making industry in Mexico as they appeared at a time of prosperity, in the late 1970s. This will be followed by a summary of the changes taking place in the political economy. Finally, the paper will note some of the tendencies now being observed within the garment industry. These suggest that the more positive conclusions drawn about the industry in times of prosperity under an import substituting regime must now be re-examined.

Rural industry: from expansion to contraction

Evidence was mounting in the 1960s and 1970s that small-scale manufacturing activities were moving out from Mexican cities to the countryside. New industries were concentrating in a broad region comprising the states of Jalisco, Michoacán and Guanajuato. By the early 1980s, some 50 to 60 small towns had come to specialize in particular industrial activities. Many branches of the garment sector were represented, as were shoemaking and food processing, leatherware and ceramics, glass-blowing and plastic bag making and the manufacture of small machine parts. While a few industries built on earlier artisan traditions, the majority were demonstrably modern (Arias, 1988; 1990). From the start they had employed a waged – largely female – labour force; they had invested regularly to up-grade workshop technology; and they had come to supply markets throughout Mexico and the southern USA.

I had selected one small sweater-producing town, Santiago in the state of Michoacán, for detailed study in 1986. The town had a population of some 9000 people; and there were 50 industrial workshops and over 200 domestic enterprises making sweaters of knitted cloth. Santiago constituted a conveniently-bounded population where one might hope to study the historical and contemporary processes underlying the trajectory of rural industrialization. There, the life histories of enterprises, workers and owners could be explored in detail from the industry's beginnings in 1960 (Wilson, 1991).

Emphasis on a single locality provided a wealth of material on local social, economic and political relations. Obviously the greatest stress was laid on internal (and by and large incremental) processes of change. The case study could be used to document the following. The study revealed more complex processes of transformation taking place in the 25-year period than is generally assumed to be the case for workshop based industry. An early industrial phase characterized by close contacts amongst workshop owners and overall clandestinity could be clearly distinguished from later phases where workshop differentiation had come to the fore, expressed particularly clearly through the differing possibilities for technological change and degree of legality. Larger workshops had been able to improve the quality of their product and so reach higher priced markets. Changes had also taken place in labour relations: from being modelled on the household they came to take a more depersonalized form. Forms of labour protest also changed. It was partly on account of labour struggle that the most profitable workshops had been pressed into paying minimum wages and social security. With the introduction of more sophisticated technology, owners were setting higher value on their workers' skills and experience.

Subsequent reflections on the pattern and history of small-scale industrialization led to more theoretical discussions concerning the clusters of small-scale industry which took as starting points concepts of flexible specialization, collective efficiency, and images of workshops as both informal and domestic domains.

The broader economic and political changes underway in Mexico during the 1980s could only be introduced into the analysis as a series of external factors. It was not possible to use the lens of a detailed case study to grasp the magnitude and irrevocability of the changes being ushered in by debt and recession. Almost inevitably too much weight was being placed on the locality and on the particularity of the society of workers and owners. Too little attention was paid to the enveloping political economy and institutional context or to the way that events taking place in the economy as a whole were provoking responses and reactions in the locality. There were both methodological advantages and disadvantages in treating a locality like Santiago as a bounded population.

Most recent studies on Mexico quote the fact that 1982 marked the onset of recession. From a perspective in small-scale industry, however, responses were lagged. The economic problems had first affected the large-scale, formal industries as well as the state sector. Many workers were being made redundant, including many organized and middle-class workers for the first time; minimum wage levels were cut and consumer demand fell. But in small-scale production, there was considerable confusion and uncertainty. After 40 years of prosperity and hope and when modernity had seemed a realizable objective, at least for the bulk of the *mestizo* population, it took time and effort for people to appreciate the extent to which their lives and livelihoods were being threatened.

At first, the small-scale producers scattered in the towns of western central Mexico had not been sure whether debt and recession represented a short-term hiccup and only a limited period of straitened economic circumstances or whether something more major was happening. In the short run, they tended to continue producing, made more efforts to find markets, tried to diversify into other garment lines and even into other economic activities, demanded higher productivity from their labour forces and pleaded for greater tolerance from buyers and creditors in order to weather the depression.

Fieldwork in Santiago had been done at a critical turning point in Mexico's economic history. The small independent producers' economy was collapsing; it had become abundantly clear from 1982 to 1986 that the fortunes of small-scale manufacturing were being reversed. Short-term survival strategies were being used up. The price of many inputs (including acrylic thread in the case of sweater production) from other industrial sectors soared wildly and sources of credit dried up, bringing the possibilities of technological upgrading to an abrupt end. The pace of innovation, whether in terms of type and quality of product, technology or managerial change, was seriously interrupted. The changes brought an end to the more progressive tendencies that had been associated with industrial expansion and quality improvement (especially technological change and the struggle by workers for minimum wages and social security).

Sweater production in Santiago ceased being particularly profitable in 1987 and production was cut and workers laid off. Some owners used their previous knowledge to make stronger efforts to export larger volumes (illegally) to US markets. Workers not only faced longer periods of unemployment and much lower purchasing power from their wages; they risked far more when they now struggled for their rights and needs. They too made use of their knowledge about distant labour markets and many more looked for temporary work in the US. Growing numbers of young women who possessed garment-making skills migrated to the US accompanied by their mothers in order to find work temporarily in the garment industry of the Los Angeles basin.

In the small garment-producing towns of the western central region, as in Guadalajara (Escobar and Martinez, 1990), the connections were becoming more apparent between economic depression and an individual search by enterprise owners and workers for closer contacts with the US through the expanded export of unregistered goods and through the changing patterns and gender composition of migration. This can be seen as a prelude and background to the later project entered into by Presidents Salinas and Bush to sign a North Atlantic Free Trade Agreement (NAFTA) between Mexico and the US, one of whose implicit objectives has been to diminish the volumes of the unregistered movement across the border.

Characteristics of the garment sector in prosperous times

Until recently, the garment sector in Latin America had not attracted much attention. This was in spite of the fact that it was usually the sector employing the largest number of workers: an estimated 15 per cent of the total labour force in the case of Mexico. Garment production has often been taken as an example of labour-intensive industry par excellence; and it is a sector strongly associated with women who constitute the main workers and consumers. One result of the superimposed images of primitive labour intensive industry and feminized industry is that thinking easily gets stuck with the idea that garment-making comprises only sweatshops and only sweated labour. The situation of both the sector and workers has been depicted as hopeless; whether in times of prosperity or recession, garment making is not assumed to vary very much.

This attribution of a timeless identity has been unfortunate. It has therefore been more difficult to unmask the extent of the variation within the garment industry, the extent of the labour protest and challenge and the scale of the technological and managerial up-grading. Thus, although the picture presented is of an industry that is backward and unresponsive to changes in demand or technology, this was not the case in Mexico.

The demand for garments, like that of other domestically produced consumer goods, rose steadily from the 1950s to the early 1980s. This was partly a result of the government's high wage policy that followed from the pacts made between the ruling PRI party (Partido de la Revolución Institutional) with organized labour but it was also a reflection of the changing needs and tastes of the fast-growing urban population. A mass market was being created for low-cost apparel in the towns. In time, demand rose for cheap fashion garments where styles changed regularly, and these were often inspired by what people saw in the mass media. Though new styles might appear to be copies of US or international fashion, Mexican touches were retained, especially in the amount and type of adornment.

Adoption of fashion clothing signified both modernity and the consumers' ability to buy new clothes once or twice a year. Depending on the particular garment, there would be spring and autumn collections; this happened first with women's clothing but it latterly also affected men's clothing. Expansion in waged employment for young women, especially in the *maquilladoras* of the Mexican border towns, in agro-business, and not least in small-scale industrial production (including the garment sector) itself, fuelled the demand for young women's clothing. Producing women's clothing had become a highly lucrative business. It was estimated that in 1985, for every peso invested in the production of women's fashion clothing, two pesos were earned; a rate of return that far exceeded the average rate of 1.3 pesos found in the manufacturing sector as a whole (as reported by the Mexican business journal, *Expansión*, January 16, 1985).

Changes were also underway in the possibilities open for small-scale production. The industrial and commercial expansion of the prosperous 1950s and 1960s had meant that many more industrial workers were becoming skilled at handling new machines and techniques. In the large clothing factories male workers gained experience in working industrial knitting looms, for example, and in repairing their machines. Some of these machines were suitable for use by small-scale enterprises. Some of those employed were prepared to stay on indefinitely as wage workers, but others resisted permanent proletarianization and hankered after the higher economic returns and greater social status associated with independent production. The way to independent production was very often through the formation of 'family' business that incorporated wives and daughters as well as male relatives.

There had always been a mass of small workshops producing garments in the cities, but the most important feature of the 1960s was that more technologically sophisticated machinery was being made increasingly available to small producers. Hire purchase schemes and many informal systems of credit (i.e. those operating outside the banking system) financed the acquisition of industrial looms and new types of sewing machine imported from Italy, Spain, Japan or East Germany. These more efficient machines were replacing the old wooden looms and simple Singer sewing machines that had been the mainstays of artisan garment production since the late 19th century. A lively second-hand trade in machinery developed as larger enterprises off-loaded older, less efficient machinery onto new entrants.

Workshop owners who were former migrants in the USA, had often brought back a vehicle – a pick-up truck – which allowed them to take charge of their own transport and sales. Thus these small producers could maintain a greater degree of autonomy or they could negotiate more favourable contracting deals with traders and middlemen from the cities. They could take their goods to the wealthier towns of the Mexican north and supply the retailers in a host of small towns throughout the country. Small producers without their own transport tended to distribute the bulk of their production through the local weekly open markets.

From the early 1960s, industries were moving out to the small towns of the western central region. Many reasons can be put forward to explain this tendency towards greater spatial dispersion in particular regions. Transport was no longer such a problem in the smaller towns, indeed congestion in the busy workshop areas of Mexico City and Guadalajara had begun to pose additional costs. A willing labour force could be found in the small towns and owners, often related by kin and fictive kin networks, had a better chance of collaborating on certain issues and of reaping benefits through greater collective efficiency (see Wilson, 1992). The vast majority of the small rural industries were 'hidden'; they were not registered and they were physically concealed. Commonly this practice has been explained with the argument that concealment is a necessary strategy in order to avoid the prying eyes of government officials trying to enforce compliance with tax and labour legislation. But a counter-argument can be proposed. Concealment also demonstrated the domestic nature and identification of industrial activities and this has been an essential element facilitating the employment of young women in the highly conservative and catholic society (Wilson, 1993).

The enterprises of the garment sector remained generally small in size. By the end of the 1970s, official statistics suggest that some 75 per cent of the registered enterprises employed only five workers or less. But, of course, the vast majority were not registered. Although the estimates are notoriously unreliable, there were possibly some three clandestine garment-making enterprises for every registered firm in the late 1970s in the cities of Guadalajara and Mexico. However, the sector was diversifying in terms of product and organization. There were some large factories employing several hundred workers (like those illegal enterprises destroyed by the 1985 earthquake in Mexico City); workshops with waged labour forces of between three and forty workers; and domestic enterprises relying primarily on family labour. All types of enterprise might put out parts of the labour process to industrial home workers.

The sector has always been extremely labour intensive and has employed many more women than men. Labour constituted some 21 per cent of total production costs in the mid 1970s, compared to an average of 16 per cent for manufacturing industry as a whole. Subcontracting has also been common; in the 1970s an estimated 70 per cent of producers were thought to have been working under some form of contract (Arias, 1988).

Seasonality and rapid fashion changes have favoured forms of organization and management associated with flexible specialization. Producers must avoid stocking garments in that those produced in one fashion season will be unsellable in the next. Collaboration amongst producers has usually been extremely important especially during the early phases of industrial growth. By clustering, specializing and sharing certain interests (especially in connection with blacklisting or disciplining 'difficult' workers, establishing informal credit systems, trying out new technology) small firms have won higher levels of overall efficiency and collective competitiveness. But as processes of differentiation got underway, so levels of direct collaboration appear to have lessened. This was especially the case when some larger enterprises in their pursuit of higher quality were forced to become more 'legal' and thus shared significantly fewer interests with the small struggling clandestine producers of shoddy goods.

The tendency towards more flexible production had repercussions on labour relations. Under one interpretation of the flexible specialization approach, it is the workers who are made 'flexible'. They are either laid off for months on end or they are pressed into working very long hours to meet rushed orders at other times of the year. Flexibility in the Mexican garment industry could, however, take on other meanings which arose from the presence of highly-skilled, versatile workers who were able to perform various parts of the labour process and work under collaborative, less confrontational relations with their employers.

The introduction of more technologically sophisticated machines in the garment sector appears to have given some advantages to labour: skilled, experienced workers became more sought after and could then insist on better employment conditions by virtue of their greater bargaining power. Technological change did open up greater possibilities for workers to see and value themselves in a different light and to fight for their right to a minimum wage and other benefits. Yet one must also remember that workshop industry was always rooted in close personal relations between workers and enterprise owners. This led to labour relations that were at one and the same time more tolerant and benevolent as well as more exploitative than in employment situations where labour relations were not founded on the idiom of kin. The Mexican expression *la cara de la comadre* (the face of the godmother) expresses this essential ambiguity.

One can claim that under the general conditions of economic growth and prosperity and with the possibilities open for periodic labour migration to the US, a progressive trajectory had been set in motion. Though the majority of garment enterprises might remain clandestine and illegal, nevertheless not only was investment occurring, so too was a movement towards greater labour skills and the payment of minimum wages. Thus over time one could see processes within the small-scale garment sector towards greater 'formalization'. This was the more positive trajectory that the country's economic crisis and subsequent restructuring interrupted.

Moving into export-driven growth

The 1980s saw the end of a long cycle of growth in Mexico based on strong state intervention and highly protectionist policies. Domestic industry was promoted through an import substitution regime of accumulation. This regime was far more determining of Mexican economic and political life than the usual term 'model' implied. Not only were Mexican industries protected, the strategy had also been partly responsible for maintaining a vast and complex array of institutions and political arrangements and alliances. The governing PRI party had since its inception entered into pacts with the private sector on the one side and with the peasants and organized labour on the other. This policy had born fruit; for around 40 years (until the late 1970s) the average rate of growth had been 6 per cent per annum and immediately before recession, it had risen to 8 per cent. General economic prosperity had been accompanied by political stability and relatively harmonious industrial and social relations.

The old economic regime had run into serious difficulties by the mid 1970s. Latterly, economic growth had been maintained temporarily on account of the oil boom (1978–81) and the massive overseas borrowing that this had allowed. Government policy clung to the belief that through loans and selective imports, a second phase of import substitution could be triggered in which Mexico would develop a much more diversified capital goods sector. But changes in the international economy brought to light the acute vulnerability of the Mexican economy. As a result of declining oil prices, rising interest rates and the large deficits appearing in Mexico's trade balance, the bubble of prosperity burst in 1982 and crisis and indebtedness followed.

The plunge into debt ushered in a period in which economic thinking in and about Mexico was totally revised. Servicing the debt was to take some 6 per cent of GDP. During President De la Madrid's administration (1982–88) the country started its structural adjustment along the lines laid down by the IMF: public social expenditure was cut; domestic prices were decontrolled; wages were controlled to reduce inflation; the currency was devalued; trade was liberalized and the privatization of inefficient state-owned enterprises was begun. During this period there were massive cutbacks in the public sector and redundancies in manufacturing industry, with more than 60,000 laid off (Alba and Roberts, 1990).

De la Madrid's policies failed to adjust the economy. Inflation worsened reaching a record low of 131.8 per cent in 1987, investment fell by an average of 4.4 per cent per annum and real wages continued to fall

(Morales, 1992). This was the bleak situation confronting Carlos Salinas when he took office in 1988. Salinas and his team have met with much greater success (and luck) than the previous administration. Prices were stabilized and a measure of confidence was restored amongst the business community.

Exports of manufactured goods grew. Major efforts were made to attract greater foreign investment and make Mexican industries more internationally competitive. And the expansion took place most strongly in the automobile and machinery sectors as well as in the in-bond assembly plants (*maquiladoras*) which grew by a factor of five, employed 500,000 workers and came to produce a quarter of the value of Mexican exports. Characteristically, it was the relatively high technology industries that were exporting most. In contrast, the export share of more labour intensive industries, notably textiles and garments, was falling fast. In 1975, garments had constituted 12 per cent of Mexican registered exports, but by 1987 the share had declined to a mere 4 per cent (Harris, 1991).

Trade liberalization was not only connected with the massive expansion of exports, it also resulted in a flood of goods imported into the country. After Mexico joined the GATT in 1986, barriers to trade were brought down at an even faster rate than required. Mexico joined the international community rapidly and abruptly, shifting from being a closed to being one of the most open economies in the world (Sandoval and Arroyo, 1990). The changes underway have been far more major and far-reaching than can be captured by the term 'adjustment'. A new regime of accumulation has been inaugurated based on closer regional ties, foreign investment, privatization, trade liberalization and export-directed growth. The next step in this process of liberalization is at present under negotiation: Mexico's pending membership of a Free Trade Agreement with the US and Canada.

As pointed out by a number of commentators (for example, Morales, 1992), Mexico's moves towards liberalization are taking place at a time when the country faces more protectionist policies from others, not least from its main trading partner, the US. This makes the future of Mexico's export policy more uncertain. In addition, thorny questions of national identity and culture are being raised. Under the new regime of accumulation, laws have been passed attacking some of the central pillars of 'Mexicanidad', for example, the current moves to end state protection to *ejidos* (Appendini, 1992). Very different institutional arrangements, policies and political scenarios are on the agenda with President Salinas de Gortari embodying the new times.

Adoption of this policy of economic restructuring is signalling the end of Mexico's position as a relatively high wage society. Comparisons with other Latin American countries suggest that Mexico suffered the most painful and rigorous restructuring seen from the point of view of labour (Escobar, 1988; Alba and Roberts, 1990). One key element of the new economic policy has been the dismantling of the protection previously given to organized labour. New agreements are being pressed upon labour unions and Mexico has been transformed from a high to a low wage economy.

Workers in the major export industries have lost least, and some may have even gained; the situation has been quite different in the informal or workshop sector which included the bulk of garment manufacture. From a survey done in 1985, Escobar (1988) estimated that the real wages of workers in workshops in Guadalajara dropped 39.9 per cent from 1982 to 1985. But differences amongst the workforce were so great that the average serves as only a rough approximation. The changes, he suggests, must be analysed along lines of sex and marital status, age, and skill. Overall women lost more than men: a drop of 45.6 per cent for women as against a drop of 38.5 per cent for men, in spite of the overall intensification of work by women in their attempt to make up for lost earning power. Among unmarried workers, men lost little (11.1 per cent) while unmarried women lost 50.8 per cent. A second survey completed in 1987 showed a deepening of the same processes that had been evident in 1985. Again women lost more than men: they lost 50 per cent in real earnings in the period 1982–87 compared to 40 per cent for men. In terms of industries, the hardest hit were the women employed in garment production; this was the case whether one considered large or small enterprises or whether they were located in Guadalajara or in a small town in the western central region.

The prospects facing garment production in the new economy

The economic and social implications of the new regime of accumulation are not yet clear or understood. But already one can observe growing polarization between the booming export industries financed increasingly by direct foreign investment and the increasingly deregulated and informalizing economy to which the garment sector clearly belongs.

There is considerable evidence to suggest that industrial activities are continuing to go ‘underground’. This means that firms that were previously registered and complying with most of the labour and tax legislations are closing down, only to re-open in the deregulated sector. Furthermore, unemployment and greater impoverishment amongst some sections of the middle classes are provoking many new groups to enter small-scale, deregulated production and open clandestine enterprises. In terms of percentage of the labour force employed, the informal industrial economy in Mexico is thought to have expanded from around 24 per cent to 33 per cent in the period 1980 to 1987 (Alba and Roberts, 1990).

The growing unregulated garment sector is facing many problems as a result of the economic transformation. First, with growing impoverishment felt especially keenly in the cities, the pattern of household expenditures amongst the popular classes is altering. A higher proportion of earnings is being devoted to buying the most essential goods: food constitutes a higher share while clothes and shoes are of lower priority. Second, trade liberalization has meant that domestic clothing producers are now facing much more serious competition from the cheap imported goods, especially from Asian countries. These tend to be distributed through the weekly open markets where they compete directly with Mexican produced clothes. But there are additional complications on account of brandname preferences: an important trade has grown in the distribution of relatively expensive imported sportswear. Items produced in Korea or Taiwan are much sought after despite their costing at least double the price of the copies locally made. Thirdly, the supply price of inputs required by the garment industry continue to increase in an erratic fashion.

Recent case study research suggests that the structure of the garment industry is undergoing a profound change and that three main elements can be distinguished (Escobar, 1988). First, subcontracting is tending to increase. Under the period of economic growth and prosperity, the market 'moved' fast. Clients paid in cash for goods, often in advance. Producers could seek out markets where money was returned quickly. This liquidity and speed gave producers a greater chance to protect their own autonomy and avoid becoming ensnared in disadvantageous subcontracting deals. In recent years, however, liquidity has diminished and this appears to have been linked with a major expansion in subcontracting whereby strong commercial interests in the cities force producers to supply goods under far less favourable and more exploitative conditions than before.

The second feature suggested is the growing informalization of the garment industry. Not only are there growing numbers of enterprises contravening the law, but the state authorities whose task it had been to uphold the labour legislation are viewing the legal situation in a different way. Thirdly, not only are enterprises moving to the unregulated sector, they are also moving location so as to start afresh in different urban or rural localities rather than remain in the well-known garment making districts in Guadalajara or Mexico City. A new phase of industrial relocation is underway and increasing numbers of new garment making activities are being taken out to the small towns of the western central region. The movement out of the cities is being attributed to the lower wage levels (some 25 per cent lower than in comparable urban enterprises) and on the greater need for physical concealment and clandestinity. Now it is suggested that the 'typical' new enterprises of the countryside are only nominally independent and that they are tied closely to the commercial concerns in the cities (Escobar, 1988; Arias, 1990).

Conclusion

The main point I have tried to make in this paper is that an assessment of the trajectory of a particular industrialization process demands that one looks at both macro tendencies and micro practices. The perspective presented here has taken issue with the usual definition given to workshop-based garment industry as comprising only 'sweatshops'. Here the protection offered domestic industry during the regime of accumulation dominating the Mexican economy for 40 years up to the early 1980s had allowed a degree of movement and development and had given workers some space in which to negotiate higher wages and better conditions. The re-direction of the political economy during the 1980s has reversed this tendency and has removed the spaces where workers could previously take action.

Notes

Preface

1. See Van Dijk and Secher Marcussen (1990) and Rassmussen *et al.* (eds) (1992).

Chapter 1

1. Localization economies are external to the firm, but internal to an industry, and urbanization economies are external to both the firm and the industry. The first results from the increased demand for goods and services from specific industries (see Cohen, 1991:34).
2. The subtitle of his book is 'Institutions of industrial restructuring'.
3. He distinguishes the entrepreneurial firm from the hierarchical firm of Chandler (1977) and Williamson (1975). Administration in a managerial hierarchy is considered an expensive way of co-ordination, which more often could take place via the market, or through consultative co-operation among mutually interdependent firms.
4. Best stresses institutional pluralism. The same positive result can be achieved through different institutional arrangements. He notably compares the different arrangements in Italy, Japan and Germany (then West Germany).
5. This is broader than Williamson (1975), who discusses only the alternatives via the market, or via hierarchies. Other modes of organization which can be mentioned are co-operative ventures and licensing.
6. Best (1990:17) notes that conventional economics, which sharply divides microeconomics from macroeconomic topics, obscures a third level of organization crucial to explaining the competitiveness of firms, namely the sector institutions or the extra-firm infrastructure.
7. Examples mentioned by Best (1990:17).
8. The hypotheses that come up immediately are: the introduction of new technologies (more flexible and computer-controlled equipment), the segmentation of major producer markets, and the increased globalization of the economy due to increased trade and improved communications.
9. The *Wall Street Journal of Europe* (November 18, 1991) notes that the process of vertical disintegration may have reached its limits in the electronics industry.
10. In these cases, the innovation process assumes somewhat different forms, and it would take us too far afield to elaborate on this here. See Hughes (1987).
11. The early field testing of a production technique which is usually associated with innovators in the North, and requires both perseverance and money mixed with a good deal of faith in the cause, is not at issue here.

Chapter 2

1. These enterprises correspond to what Helmsing (1991), in his study of rural industries in Zimbabwe, calls 'Type II enterprises'.
2. Most of the building material production is in non-metallic mineral and metal products which, according to Riddell (1990), employed 41,500 in total.
3. A more detailed account of this sector study is given in Pedersen (1992a). The fieldwork was carried out in 1990.

4. The building sector study was carried out by Jesper Rasmussen and published in Rasmussen (1992a). A short version is presented in Rasmussen (1992b). The field work was carried out in 1989.
5. The fieldwork was carried out in the beginning of 1992.
6. There are only a few dressmaking enterprises operated by women in the two business centres; however, such enterprises are most likely operated in the residential areas of the towns, which we have not investigated.
7. A more detailed account of these training centres is given in Pedersen (1992b).
8. Wages in the small workshops vary from Z$150–250 per month, while they are around Z$375 in the industry.

Chapter 4

1. See the introductory chapter.
2. For the definition of these terms see the introduction.
3. For example, Holmstrom and Tirole (1989) for a summary of these approaches and Williamson (1989) for a summary of the contractual approach taken by transaction cost economics.
4. Informalization of the labour force can be the result of four different processes (Mendez-Rivero, 1991:78):
   1. As the result of a strategy of externalization of the cost function by larger enterprises to overcome a situation of profit squeeze, or to recuperate a falling rate of profit.
   2. Informalization of value added by sharing parts of the production process between the larger and a number of microenterprises. The arguments are: lower necessary investments, higher competition and more specialization.
   3. Informalization of the market, where demand changes in favour of products and services provided by microenterprises.
   4. Informalization as the result of introducing new and flexible technologies.
5. In Indonesia no original industry-level data were collected, but the character of the industrialization process comes out very clearly in studies e.g. Hill (1990) and Mackaaij (1991).
6. In the seventies the country still stressed import-substitution and these industries were often protected by imposing tariffs and setting quotas. Non-tariff barriers (NTBs) were created by making regulations more complex and using licensing in a restrictive manner. In the eighties the policy changed to an export-promotion strategy.
7. For a detailed assessment, see Mackaaij (1991), who concluded that 1992 was not really threatening for Indonesia.
8. Will there be a limited number of other blocks, such as one around Japan, one in America with the USA, Mexico and Canada and one in the Middle East? In that case, what would Indonesia's role be in a block dominated by Japan?
9. Except by the so-called new-institutionalists. See Booij (1987).

Chapter 5

1. The data for this paper was collected from November 1990 up to May 1991, within the framework of the project 'Impact of Technological and Organizational Changes on Women's Employment in the Leather Footwear Industry in India', being carried out by the Department of Human Geography, University of Amsterdam, the Netherlands and the Central Leather Research Institute in Madras, India. The project as a whole is financed by the Netherlands's Minister for Development Cooperation. Additional funding was provided by the

Netherlands Foundation for the Advancement of Tropical research (WOTRO). Acknowledgements go to: Director CLRI, Dr. K. Seshagiri Rao, B. Krishnama Naidu, C. Pulinda Rao, Vikrant Shastri, Mahender Solanki, Isa Baud, Martin Klapwijk, Henk Kox, Hubert Schmitz and Hermine Weijland.

Government policy is not touched upon in this paper. Policies regarding the footwear sector were dominated by regulations, reservations and restrictions. However, the new Government that took office in June 1991 has started a campaign of deregulation and liberalization. At this moment it is very hard to assess the present policy environment.

2. The other main footwear centres are Madras and its hinterland, Kanpur, Calcutta and the so-called Kolhapuri belt in South Maharashtra and North Karnataka.
3. This market seems to have completely collapsed in 1991.
4. In their book on the new institutional economics, Zukin and DiMaggio suggest that given the inability of the concepts of market and hierarchy to capture the (frequent) occurrence of ongoing relationships of trust and mutual dependency, there is '. . . a need for a third ideal-type decision structure, based on informal social relations, parallel to markets and firms' (Zukin and DiMaggio, 1990: 9). Best (1990) and Powell (1989) argue that the dichotomy cannot capture the complexities of competition and institutional dynamics in real-life economic exchange. Several articles collected in Thompson *et al.* (1991) come to the same conclusion.
5. One of the few comprehensive treatments on the concept of trust can be found in Gambetta (1988).
6. Coming from another angle, the theory of repeated games and supergames, in which players accept a long-run average pay-off, explains that co-operation develops among players, even irrespective of the initial presence or absence of trust (Axelrod, 1984; Mertens, 1989).
7. Of course there are also internal conflicts of interest in the Third Italy, but they are not along one general chasm, as in this case. See also Piore and Sabel (1984), for cases of the strength of ethnic groups to pursue a strategy of flexible specialization.

Chapter 7

1. The paper has benefited from the contributions of M. Klapwijk, P. Knorringa and A. Leliveld.
2. In Indonesia, cottage industry is defined as family enterprises with less than five workers.
3. Most of the given examples are taken from Asheim (1992:47–9).
4. Number obtained from Ministry of Industry.
5. See data sources attached to Table 1.
6. This grouping follows a leading study on economic diversity in Indonesia (Hill, 1989). Two provinces were excluded: DKI Jakarta because of its city characteristics, and East Timor because of data deficiencies.
7. Excluding the province of Jakarta.
8. Poverty incidence data are taken from a 1980 survey. Data from 1987 are rejected to avoid circular reasoning: poverty affects inputs, but low inputs again lead to poverty! It therefore was assumed that persistent poverty as reflected by 1980 data would cause high participation in RCI.
9. A more rigorous statistical analysis including two independent sets of data for 25 provinces is presented in Weijland, 1991.

Chapter 9

1. Many people and institutions have contributed to the success of this research. Among them we wish to thank Frances Stewart, Hubert Schmitz, Peter Knorringa and Eduardo Zepeda for helpful comments on an earlier version of this paper; the *Camara del Calzado* of Guadalajara and Leon for their organizational support during the field work in Mexico. Financial support from the Instituto Tecnologico de Monterrey is gratefully acknowledged.

   The two case studies in Italy are the area of Fermo and Macerata in Marche (Centre) and the Brenta area in Veneto (north-east). In Mexico the study has been carried out in Guadalajara (Jalisco) and Leon (Guanajuato).
2. The data are estimates supplied by the Camara de la Industria del Calzado del Estado de Guanajuato.
3. A very similar questionnaire has been also adopted to interview 50 enterprises in Italy (30 in Marche and 20 in the Brenta area).
4. For the footwear industry the tariff was almost halved from 35 per cent to 17 per cent of import value and all import licenses were eliminated (CANAICAL, 1991).
5. In 1989 the USA consumed 1393 millions of pairs of shoes and 82 per cent were imported (ILO, 1992).
6. The *maquilladora* or in-bond processing industry has flourished in Mexico since 1982. At the end of 1990 there were 1795 businesses in operation, employing 450,000 people and located both in the traditional border areas and in some new zones of the interior. The principal activities are the assembly of automobiles, electrical goods, electronics, furniture, chemicals and textiles. The *maquilladoras* account for over 70 per cent of foreign investments in the country (Economist Intelligence Unit, 1992).
7. Consumer prices rose by 3811 per cent in 1983–88. However, from 1988 thanks to the success of the Pacto de Solidaridad Economica introduced in December 1987, inflation started to decelerate and in 1989 the yearly rate was reduced to 19.7 per cent, but increased to 26.7 per cent in 1990 (Economist Intelligence Unit, 1992).

References

Preface

Rasmussen, J., Schmidt, H., and Van Dijk, M.P., (1992), 'Introduction: Exploring a new approach to small-scale industry', *IDS Bulletin*, Vol. 23, No. 3.

Van Dijk, M.P. and Secher Marcussen, H., (eds) (1990), *Industrialization in the Third World: The need for alternatives*, F. Cass, London.

Chapter 1

Bagachwa, M.S.D., (1992), 'Choice of Technology in Small and Large Firms: Grain Milling in Tanzania', in *World Development*, Vol.20, No. 1, pp. 97–107.

Bain, J.S., (1956), *Barriers to New Competition: Their character and consequences in manufacturing industries*, Harvard University Press, Cambridge.

Best, M.H., (1990), *The New Competition: Institutions of Industrial Restructuring*, Harvard University Press, Cambridge.

Bijker, W.E., Hughes, T.P. and Pinch, T. (eds) (1987), *The Social Construction of Technology: New directions in the sociology and history of technology*, MIT Press, Cambridge.

Callon, M., (1987), *Society in the Making: The study of technology as a tool for sociological analysis*, in Bijker *et al.*

Chandler, A.D., (1977), *The Visible Hand*, Harvard University Press, Cambridge.

Cohen, M.A., (1991), *Urban Policy and Economic Development: An agenda for the 1990s*, IBRD, Washington.

Hakansson, H., (ed.) (1987) 'Product Development in Networks' in H. Hakansson, *Industrial Technological Development*, Croom Helm, London, pp.84–127.

Hirst, P. and Zeitlin, J., (1991), 'Flexible Specialization versus Post-Fordism' in *Economy and Society*, Vol.20, No.1, Feb., pp.1–55.

Hughes, Thomas P., (1987), 'The Evolution of Large Technological Systems', in Bijker *et al.*

Kaplinsky, R., (1990), *The Economies of Small: Appropriate technology in a changing world*, IT Publications in association with Appropriate Technology International, London.

Laage-Hellman, J. (1989), *Technological Development in Industrial Networks*, Acta Universitatis Uppsaliensis No.16, Uppsala.

Pedersen, P.O., (1986), 'The role of business services in regional development – a new growth centre strategy?' *Scandinavian Housing and Planning Research*, 3, pp.167–182.

Piore, M. and Sabel, C.F. (1984), *The Second Industrial Divide, Possibilities for Prosperity*, Basic books, New York.

Pyke, F., Becattini, G., and Sengenberger, W. (1990), (eds), *Industrial districts and interfirm cooperation in Italy*, International Institute for Labour Studies, Geneva.

Pyke, F. and Sengenberger, W., (1992), *Industrial districts and local economic regeneration*, International Institute for Labour Studies, Geneva.

Rasmussen, J., Schmitz, H. and Van Dijk, M.P., (1992), 'Introduction: Exploring a new approach to small-scale industry', *IDS Bulletin* Vol.23, No.3.

Salais, R. and Storper, M., (1992), 'The four "worlds" of contemporary industry', *Cambridge Journal of Economics* 16, pp.169–193.

Schmitz, H., (1989), 'Flexible Specialisation, A New Paradigm of Small-Scale Industrialisation?' IDS Discussion paper 261, Sussex.

Schmitz, H., (1990), 'Small firms and flexible specialization in developing countries', *Labour and society*. Vol.15, No.3.

Scott, J., (1988), 'Trend Report: Social Network Analysis', in *Sociology*, Vol.22, No.1.

Smillie, I., (1991), *Mastering the Machine: Poverty, Aid and Technology*, Intermediate Technology Publications, London.

Sverrisson, A., (1993), *Evolutionary Technical Change and Flexible Mechanization: Entrepreneurship and Industrialization in Kenya and Zimbabwe*, Lund University Press.

Van Dijk, M.P., (1992a), 'How Relevant is Flexible Specialization in Burkina Faso's Informal Sector and the Formal Manufacturing Sector?' in *IDS Bulletin*, Vol.23, No.3.

Van Dijk, M.P., (1992b), *The Interrelations between Industrial Districts and Technological Capacities Development*, UNCTAD, Geneva.

Williamson, O., (1975), *Markets and Hierarchies, Analysis and Antitrust Implications: A Study of the Economics of Internal Organization*. The Free Press, New York.

Williamson, O., (1989), 'Transaction Cost Economics', in Schmalensee and Willig (see p. 167).

Chapter 2

Aeroe, A., (1992), *Rethinking Industrialization – from a national to a local perspective.* CDR Project Paper 9.23. Centre for Development Research, Copenhagen.

Christensen, P.R., Eskelinen, H., Forsström, B., Lindmark, L. and Vatne, E., (1990), 'Firms in networks: Concepts, spatial impacts and policy implications', *NordReFo* 1990. 1, pp.11–58.

Colclough, C., (1991), 'Structuralism vs Neo-liberalism: An introduction', in C. Colclough and J. Manor (eds), *States or Markets? Neo-liberalism and the development policy debate*, Clarendon Press, Oxford.

Government of the Republic of Zimbabwe, (1991), *The promotion of investment policy and regulations*, Harare.

GEMINI, (1991), *Micro and Small-scale Enterprises in Zimbabwe: Results of a Country-wide Survey*, GEMINI Technical Report 25, Bethesda, Maryland.

Helmsing, A.H.J., (1991), 'Rural industries and growth points: Issues in an ongoing debate', in N.D. Mutizwa-Mangiza and A.H.J. Helmsing (eds) *Rural Development and Planning in Zimbabwe*, Avebury, Aldershot, UK.

Johanson, J. and Mattson, L.G., (1986), 'Inter-organizational relations in industrial systems – a network approach compared with the transaction cost approach', *International Studies of Management and Organization*. Vol.40, No.2.

Pedersen, P.O., (1992a), 'Agricultural marketing and processing in small towns in Zimbabwe – Gutu and Gokwe', in J. Baker and P.O. Pedersen (eds), *The rural-urban interface in Africa: Expansion and adaption.* Scandinavian Institute for African Studies, Uppsala.

Pedersen, P.O., (1992b) 'Private sector contributions to vocational training in Zimbabwe's district service centres', paper presented to seminar on state and non-state provision of services in Eastern African and South Asia, June 15–17, 1992, Centre for Development Research, Copenhagen.

Pedersen, P.O., (1992c), 'Entrepreneurs and managers in Zimbabwe's district service centres', *Entrepreneurship and Regional Development*, 4, pp.57–72.

Pedersen, P.O., (1989), *The role of small enterprises and small towns in the developing countries – and in the developed*, CDR Project Paper 89.1, Centre for Development Research, Copenhagen.

Rasmussen, J., (1992a), *The local entrepreneurial milieu. Enterprise networks in small Zimbabwean towns*, Research Report No. 79, Department of Geography, Roskilde University in co-operation with Centre for Development Research, Copenhagen.

Rasmussen, J., (1992b), 'The small enterprise environment in Zimbabwe: Growing in the shadow of the large enterprises', *IDS Bulletin*. Vol.23, No.3, pp.21–27.

Rasmussen, J., Schmitz, H. and Van Dijk, M.P., (1992), 'Introduction: Exploring a new approach to small-scale industry', *IDS Bulletin*, Vol. 23, No. 3, pp.2–7

Republic of Zimbabwe, (1991), *Second five-year national development plan 1991–1995*, Harare.

Riddell, R.C. *et al.*, (1990), *Manufacturing Africa: Performance and prospects of seven countries in Sub-Saharan Africa*, James Currey, London.

Schmitz, H. (1990), 'Small firms and flexible specialization in developing countries', *Labour and Society*, Vol.5, No.3, pp.257–285.

Chapter 3

Bagachwa, M.S.D. (1992), 'Choice of Technology in Small and Large Firms: Grain Milling in Tanzania', in *World Development*, Vol.20, No.1, pp.97–107.

Evans, P. and Stephens J.D., (1988), 'Studying development since the sixties: The emergence of a new comparative political economy', in *Theory and Society*, 17, pp.713–745.

Kaplinsky, R., (1990), *The Economies of Small: Appropriate technology in a changing world*, Intermediate Technology Publications in association with Appropriate Technology International, London.

Mouzelis, N.P., (1988), 'Sociology of Development: Reflections on the Present Crisis', in *Sociology*, Vol.22, No.1, February, pp.23–44.

Smillie, I., (1991), *Mastering the Machine: Poverty, Aid and Technology*, Intermediate Technology Publications, London.

Stinchcombe, A.L., (1978), *Theoretical Methods in Social History*, Academic Press, London.

Chapter 4

Bain, J.S., (1956), *Barriers to New Competition: Their character and consequences in manufacturing industries*, Harvard University Press, Cambridge.

Best, M.H., (1990), *The New Competition: Institutions of industrial restructuring*, Harvard University Press, Cambridge.

Booij, H., (1987), 'New Institutional Economics' (in Dutch), in H.W. Lambers en L.H. Klaassen (eds) *Van alle markten thuis*, Universiteitspers, Rotterdam.

Caves, R.E., (1989), 'International differences in industrial organization', in R. Schmalensee and R.D. Willig (eds).

Davies, S. and Lyonds, B., (eds) (1988), *Economics of industrial Organisation*, Longman, London.

Goodman, E. and Bamford, J., (eds) (1989) *Small Firms and Industrial Districts in Italy*, Routledge, London.

Green, C., (1987), 'Industrial organization paradigms, Empirical evidence and the case for competition policy', in *Canadian Journal of Economics*, Vol.XX, No.3.

Hill, H., (1990), 'Indonesia's industrial transformation', in *Bulletin of Indonesian Economic Studies*, Vol.26, No.2.

Holmstrom, B.R. and Tirole, J., (1989), 'The theory of the firm', in R. Schmallensee and R.D. Willig (eds).

Kay, J.A., (1991), 'Economics and business' in *Economic Journal*, Vol.101, No.404.

Mackaaij, M.G., (1991), *Trade Relations between Indonesia and the Netherlands after 1992*, MA thesis, Erasmus University, Rotterdam.

Marshall, A., (1992), *Principles of Economics*, Macmillan, London.

Mendez-Rivero, D., (1991), *Informalization of the Venezuelan Labour Force*, ISS, The Hague.

Piore, M. and Sabel, C.F., (1984), *The Second Industrial Divide: Possibilities for prosperity*, Basic Books, New York.

Pyke, F., Becattini, G. and Sengenberger, W., (eds) (1990), *Industrial Districts and Inter-firm Cooperation in Italy*, IILS, Geneva.

Rasmussen, J., Schmitz, H. and Van Dijk, M.P., (eds) (1992, 'Flexible specialisation: a new view on small industry?' *IDS Bulletin*, Vol.23, No.3, July.

Schmallensee, R. and Willig, R.D. (eds), (1989), *Handbook of Industrial Organization*, Vols I, II. North-Holland, Amsterdam.

Scherer, F., (1970), *Industrial Market Structure and Economic Performance*, Rand McNally, Chicago.

Schmitz, H., (1992), 'On the clustering of firms', in J. Rasmussen *et al.*, (eds).

Tirole, J., (1990), *The Theory of Industrial Organization*, MIT Press, Cambridge.

UNIDO, (1985), *L'industrialisation au Burkina Faso*, United Nations Industrial Development Organisation, Vienna.

Van Dijk, M.P., (1990), 'Burkina Faso, Favouring modern medium scale enterprises', in M.P. Van Dijk and H. Secher Marcussen (eds).

Van Dijk, M.P., (1991), *The Dynamics of the Informal Sector in Ouagadougou, Burkina Faso*. IBRD, Washington.

Van Dijk, M.P., (1992a), 'How relevant is flexible specialisation in Burkina Faso's informal sector and the formal manufacturing sector?' in J. Rasmussen *et al.* (eds).

Van Dijk, M.P. and Secher Marcussen, H., (eds) (1990), *Industrialization in the Third World: The need for alternatives*, F. Cass, London.

Van Dijk, M.P. and Kameo, D., (1991), *Industrialization in Indonesia*, Working paper No. 6, Universitas Kristen Satya Wacana, Salatiga.

Van Dijk, M.P., Asselbergs, G. and Sleuwaegen, L. (1992), Vertical Disintegration in the European Automobile Industry, ECOZOEK dag, Rotterdam.

Williamson, O., (1975), *Markets and Hierarchies, Analysis and Antitrust Implications: A study of the economics of internal organization*, The Free Press, New York.

Williamson, O., (1989), 'Transaction cost economics', in R. Schmalensee and R.D. Willig (eds).

World Bank, (1991), *World Development Report 1991*, IBRD, Washington.

Chapter 5

Asheim, B.T., (1992), 'Flexible specialisation, Industrial Districts and Small Firms: A critical appraisal', in H. Ernste and V. Meier (eds) *Regional Development and Contemporary Industrial Response: Extending Flexible Specialisation*, Belhaven Press, London.

Axelrod, R., (1984), *The evolution of cooperation*, Basic Books, New York.

Best, M.H., (1990), *The New Competition: Institutions of Industrial Restructuring*, Polity Press, Cambridge.

Boomgard, J.J., Davies, S.P., Haggblade, S.J., and Mead, D.C., (1992), 'A Subsector Approach to Small Enterprise Promotion and Research', *World Development*, Vol.20, No.2, pp.199–212.

Braddach, J.L. and Eccles, R.G., (1989), 'Price, Authority and Trust: From ideal types to plural forms', in *Annual Review of Sociology*, Vol. 15, pp. 97–118.

Gambetta, D. (ed.), (1988), *Trust: Making and breaking cooperative relations*, Basil Blackwell, New York.

Khare, R.S., (1984), *The Untouchable as Himself: Ideology, Identity, and Pragmatism among the Lucknow Chamars*, Oxford University Press, New York.

Knorringa, P., (1991), *Small Enterprises in the Indian Footwear Industry. A Case Study of the Agra Cluster*. Report to the Ministry of Development Cooperation. University of Amsterdam.

Knorringa, P. and Kox, H., (1992), *Transaction Regimes: An Instrument for Research in Industrial Organization*, Research Memorandum 1992–34, Faculty of Economics and Econometrics, Free University, Amsterdam.

Knorringa, P. and Weijland, H., (1992), 'Subcontracting – the Incorporation of Small Producers in Dynamic Industrial Networks', in I.S.A. Baud (ed.) *Gender, Small-Scale Industry and Development Policy*, Intermediate Technology Publications, London, pp.35–46.

Leest, G.A., (1984), *The Trade-, (Sub)contracting-, and Employment Relations in the Small Scale Footwear Industry of Agra, India*, Erasmus University, Rotterdam (mimeograph).

Lynch, O.M., (1969), *The Politics of Untouchability*, Columbia University Press, New York.

Mead, D.C., (1984), 'Of contracts and subcontracts: Small firms in vertically dis-integrated production/distribution systems in LDCs', *World Development*, Vol.12, No.11/12, pp.1095–1106.

Mertens, J.F., (1989), 'Repeated games' and 'Supergames', in J. Eatwell, M. Milgate and P. Newman (eds), *Game theory, The New Palgrave*, MacMillan, London.

Misra, S., (1980), 'Living and working conditions of labourers in leather industry in Agra', PhD on file, Institute of Social Studies, Agra University.

Powell, W.W., (1989), 'Neither market nor hierarchy: network forms of organization, in *Research in Organizational Behaviour*, Vol.12, pp.295–336.

Pyke, F., Becattini, G. and Sengenberger, W. (eds), (1990), *Industrial districts and inter-firm co-operation in Italy*, International Institute for Labour Studies, Geneva.

Schmitz, H., (1982), 'Growth constraints on small-scale manufacturing in developing countries: a critical view', *World Development*, Vol.10, No.6, pp.429–450.

Schmitz, H., (1992), On the Clustering of Small Firms, *IDS Bulletin*, Vol.23, No.3, pp.64–69.

Sharma, S.K., (1986), *The Chamar Artisans: Industrialisation, Skills and Social Mobility*, B.R. Publishing Corporation, New Delhi.

Smyth, I., (1991), 'Collective Efficiency and Selective Benefits: The Growth of the Rattan Industry of Tegalwangi (Indonesia)', *IDS Bulletin*, Vol.23, No.3, pp.51–56.

Thompson, G., Frances, J., Levacic, R. and Mitchell, J. (eds), (1991), *Markets, hierarchies and networks*, Sage Publications, London.

Williamson, O.E., (1975), *Markets and Hierarchies*, The Free Press, New York.

Williamson, O.E., (1985), *The Economic Institutions of Capitalism: Firms, Markets, Relational Contracting*, The Free Press, New York.

Williamson, O.E. and Ouchi, W.G., (1981), 'The markets and hierarchies program of research: origins, implications, prospects', in A.H. van de Ven and W.F. Joyce (eds) *Perspectives on Organization Design and Behavior*, John Wiley and Sons, New York, pp.347–370.

Zukin, S. and DiMaggio, P., (1990), 'Introduction', in S. Zukin and P. DiMaggio (eds), *Structures of Capital. The Social Organization of the Economy*, Cambridge University Press, Cambridge, pp.1–36.

Chapter 6

Boomgard, J., Davies, S., Haggblade, S. and Mead, D., (1992), 'A Subsector Approach to Small Scale Enterprise Promotion and Research', in *World Development*, Vol.20, No.2, pp.199–212.

Knorringa, P. and Sandee, H., (1990), 'Changes in the Organization of Marketing and Production in Rural Industry. The Consequences of Technological Innovation on the Development of the Roof Tile Industry in Karanggeneng', Faculty of Economics, Universitas Kristen Satya Wacana, Salatiga.

Lestariyo, A.J. and Sandee, H., (1989), 'Differentiation among Rural Industrial Producers. Results of a Survey in the Boyolali Regency', Faculty of Economics, Universitas Kristen Satya Wacana, Salatiga.

Liedholm, C. and Mead, D., (1987) 'Small Scale Industries in Developing Countries: Empirical Evidence and Policy Implications', International Development paper No.9, Michigan State University.

Rasmussen, J., (1992), 'The Small Enterprise Environment in Zimbabwe: Growing in the Shadow of Large Enterprises', in *IDS Bulletin*, Vol.23, No.3, pp.21–27.

Sandee, H., (1990), 'Step by Step Innovation in Rural Industry.' Paper prepared for seminar at the National Institute for Sciences (LIPI), Jakarta, May.

Smyth, I., (1990), 'The Rattan Industry of Tegalwangi: A Success Story for Small Scale Enterprise?', Discussion Paper, Institute of Social Studies, The Hague.

White, B., (1992), 'Workshops and Factories: Dynamics of Production and Employment in West Java's Rural Footwear Industries', Research Seminar Rural Development Series, Institute of Social Studies, The Hague.

Chapter 7
Alexander, J. and Alexander, P., (1991), 'Trade and Petty Commodity Production in Early Twentieth Century Kebumen', in P. Alexander *et al.*, pp.70–91.

Alexander, J. and Alexander, P., (1990), *The Cultural Construction of Information in Javanese Markets*, Discussion paper, CASA, Amsterdam.

Alexander, P., Boomgaard, P. and White, B. (eds), (1991), *In the Shadow of Agriculture; Non-Farm Activities in the Javanese Economy, Past and Present*, Royal Tropical Institute, Amsterdam.

Anderson, D., (1982), 'Small industry in Developing Countries: a Discussion of Issues', *World Development* 10/11, pp.913–48.

Asheim, B.T., (1992), 'Flexible Specialization, Industrial Districts and Small Firms: A Critical Appraisal', in H. Ernste and V. Meier (eds) (1992), *Regional Development and Contemporary Industrial Response: Extending Flexible Specialisation*, Belhaven Press, London, pp.45–63.

Best, M.H., (1990), *The New Competition*, Polity Press, Cambridge.

BPS (Biro Pusat Statistik, Jakarta) (1987), *Supas 1985*.

—1989a, *Home Industry Statistics, 1986.*

—1989b, *Home Industry Statistics, 1987.*

—1989c, *Expenditure for Consumption of Indonesian Population by Province 1987.*

—1989d, *Statistik Indonesia 1988.*

—1989e, *Provincial Income in Indonesia, 1983–1986.*

Farbman, M. and Lessik, A., (1989), 'The Impact of Classification on Policy', in A. Gosses *et al.*, (eds), *Small Enterprises, New Approaches*, The Hague, Ministry of Foreign Affairs, pp.105–122.

Haggblade, S., Hazel, P. and Brown, J., (1989), 'Farm-Nonfarm Linkages in Rural Sub-Saharan Africa', *World Development*. Vol.17, No.8, pp.1173–1201.

Hill, H., (ed.), (1989), *Unity and Diversity: Regional Economic Development in Indonesia since 1970*, Oxford UP, Singapore.

Knorringa, P. and Weijland, H., (1993), 'Subcontracting, or the Incorporation of Small Producers in Large Networks', in I.S.A. Baud (ed.) *Women, Small Scale Industry and Development*, Intermediate Technology Publications, London.

Levitsky, J. (ed.), (1989), *Microenterprises in Developing Countries: Papers and proceedings of an international conference held in Washington*, Intermediate Technology Publications, London.

Lewis, W.A., (1954), 'Economic Development with Unlimited Supplies of Labour', *Manchester School* 26, pp.1–31.

Moser, C., (1978), 'Informal Sector or Petty Commodity Production: Dualism or Dependence in Urban Development', *World Development* Vol.6, pp.1041–64.

Oshima, H.T., (1983), 'The Transition to an Industrial Economy in Monsoon Asia', Asian Development Bank, Manila, Staff Paper 21.

Ranis, G., (1990), 'Rural Linkages and Choice of Technology', in F. Stewart *et al.* (eds), *The Other Policy*, Intermediate Technology Publications, London, pp.43–57.

Rasmussen, J., (1992), 'The Small Enterprise Environment in Zimbabwe: Growing in the Shadow of Large Enterprises', *IDS Bulletin*, pp.21–27.

Sandee, H. and Weijland, H., (1989), 'Rural Cottage Industry in Transition: Roof Tiles Industry in the Regency Boyolali, Central Java', *Bulletin of Indonesian Economic Studies*, Aug.

Schmitz, H., (1989), *Flexible Specialization – a New Paradigm of Small-Scale Industrialization?*, Discussion Paper 261, Institute of Development Studies.

Smyth, I., (1990), 'Collective Efficiency and Selective Benefits: The Growth of the Rattan Industry of Tegalwangi (Indonesia)', *IDS Bulletin*, The Hague, pp.51–56.

Stewart, F. and Ranis, G., (1990), 'Macro Policies for Appropriate Technology', in F. Stewart *et al.* pp.3–42.

Stewart, F., Thomas, H. and de Wilde, T., (eds), (1990), *The Other Policy; The influence of policies on technology choice and small enterprise development*, Intermediate Technology Publications, London.

UNDP, DGIS, ILO and UNIDO, (1988), *Development of Rural Small Industrial Enterprises*, UNIDO, Vienna.

Weijland, H., (1991), *Middlemen's Role in Rural Industry*, Research Memorandum 1991–19. Vrije Universiteit, Amsterdam.

White, B., (1992), *Workshops and Factories: Dynamics of Production and Employment in West Java's Rural Footwear Industries*, Seminar paper for Institute of Social Studies, The Hague, September 1992.

World Bank, (1990), *Indonesia, Poverty Assessment and Strategy Report*, Washington DC.

Chapter 8

Amin, A. and Robin, K., (1990), 'The re-emergence of regional economies?: the mythical geography of flexible accumulation', *Society and Space*, Vol.8.

Cho, Myung-Rae, (1991a), *Political Economy of Regional Differentiation: The state, accumulation and the regional question*, Hanul, Seoul.

Cho, Myung-Rae, (1991b), 'Peripheral post-Fordism and regional restructuring in South Korea', *World Capitalism and Korean Society*, Hanul, Seoul, (in Korean).

Coirat, B., (1991), 'Technical flexibility and mass production: flexible specialisation and dynamic flexibility', in G. Benko, and M. Dunford (eds), *Industrial Change and Regional Development: Transformation of new industrial spaces*, Belhaven Press, London.

Dunford, M., (1991), 'Industrial paradigms and social structures in areas of new industrial growth', in G. Benko and M. Dunford (eds), *Industrial Change and Regional Development: Transformation of new industrial spaces*, Belhaven Press, London.

Leborgne, D. and Lipietz, A., (1988), 'New technologies, new modes of regulation: some spatial implications', *Society and Space*, Vol.6, No.3.

Lee, Y.S., (1989), 'Industrial Subcontracting and the Structural Capacities of Working Class: the Cases of Automobile and Electronics Industries', unpublished MA thesis of the University of Ehwa, Seoul, Korea, (in Korean).

Martinelli, F. and Schoenberger, E., (1991), 'Oligopoly is alive and well: notes for a broader discussion of flexible accumulation', in G. Benko and M. Dunford (eds), *Industrial Change and Regional Development: Transformation of new industrial spaces*, Belhaven Press, London.

Park, S.O., (1991), 'High-technology industries in Korea: spatial linkages and policy implication', *Geoforum*, Vol.22, No.4.

Piore, M.J. and Sabel, C.F., (1984), *The Second Industrial Divide*, Basic Books, New York.

Sayer, A. and Walker, R., (1992), *The New Social Economy: Rethinking the division of labour*, Blackwell, Cambridge.

Schmitz, H., (1989), 'Flexible specialization: a new paradigm of small-scale industrialization?', Discussion Paper 261, Institute of Development Studies, Sussex.

Chapter 9

Becattini, G., (1989), 'Sectors and/or districts: some remarks on the conceptual foundations of industrial economics' in E. Goodman and F. Bamford (eds), *Small Firms and Industrial Districts in Italy*, Routledge, London.

Becattini, G., (1990), 'The Marshallian Industrial District as a Socio-Economic Notion', in F. Pyke *et al.*

Boston Consulting Group, (1988), 'Industria del Calzado', mimeo, Mexico City.

Brusco, S., (1990), 'The idea of the industrial district: its genesis', in F. Pyke *et al.*

CANAICAL, (1991), 'Estudio tecnico sobre el dano a la industria nacional del calzado por el incremento en las importaciones', mimeo, Mexico City.

CICEG, (1990), 'Perfil de la Industria del Calzado en México', *Calzavance*, September.

Dominguez-Villalobos, L. and Brown-Grossman, F., (1992), 'Employment and income effects of structural and technological changes in footwear manufacturing in Mexico', World Employment Programme Research Working Paper No. 224, International Labour Office, Geneva.

Economist Intelligence Unit, (1992), *Mexico, Country Profile 1991–92*, The Economist Intelligence Unit, London.

ILO, (1992), *Recent Developments in the Leather and Footwear Industry*, Fourth Tripartite Technical Meeting for the Leather and Footwear Industry, Reports I and II, International Labour Office, Geneva.

Prochnik, V., (1992), 'Spurious flexibility: technical modernisation and social inequalities in the Brasilian footwear industry', World Employment Programme Research Working Paper No. 222, International Labour Office, Geneva.

Pyke, F., Becattini, G. and Sengenberger, W., (eds), (1990), *Industrial Districts and Inter-Firm Co-operation in Italy*, International Labour Organisation (International Institute for Labour Studies), Geneva.

SECOFI, (1992), 'Programa para pomover la competitivadad e internacionalizacion de la industria de la curtiduria y del calzado', mimeo, Mexico City.

Schmitz, H., (1990), 'Small Firms and Flexible Specialisation in Developing Countries', *Labour and Society*, Vol.15, No.3.

Schmitz, H., (1992), 'On the Clustering of Firms', *IDS Bulletin*, Vol.23, No.3, July.

Chapter 10

Carlos Alba V. and Roberts, B., (1990), 'Crisis, ajuste y empleo en Mexico: la industria manufacturera de Jalisco', *Estudios Sociologicos*, Vol.VII, No.24.

Appendini, K., (1992), 'From crisis to restructuring: The debate on the Mexican economy during the 1980s.' CDR Project Paper 92, Centre for Development Research, Copenhagen.

Arias, P., (1988), 'La pequena empresa en el occidente rural', *Estudios Sociologicos*, Vol.VI, No.22.

Arias, P., (1990), 'Los talleres en el campo', *Cuadernos*, No.11–12.

Escobar, A.L., (1988), 'The rise and fall of an urban labour market: economic crisis and the fate of small workshops in Guadalajara, Mexico', *Bulletin of Latin American Research*, Vol.7, No.2.

Escobar, A.L. and Martinez C.M. de la O., (1990), 'Small-scale industry and international migration in Guadalajara, Mexico', Commission for the Study of International Migration and Co-operative Economic Development, Washington, Working paper, No.53, July.

Harris, N., (1991), 'Manufactured exports and newly industrialised countries: Mexican trade and Mexico-US economic relations', *Economic and Political Weekly*, Vol.XXVI, Nos.11/12, March.

Morales, I., (1992), 'Mexico: the making of a new pattern of governability', Paper to Seminar on Latin American Development Debates, Centre for Development Research, Copenhagen, March.

Sandoval, M.L. and Arroyo, F., (1990), 'The Mexican economy at the end of the century', *CEPAL Review*, Santiago, Chile, No.42, December.

Wilson, F., (1991), *Sweaters: gender, class and workshop-based industry in Mexico*, Macmillan International Political Economy Series.

Wilson, F., (1992), 'Modern workshops industry in Mexico: On its way to collective efficiency?' *IDS Bulletin*, Sussex.

Wilson, F., (1993), 'Workshops as domestic domains: Reflections on small-scale industry in Mexico', *World Development*, Vol.21, No.1.